VOLUPTUOUS LIES

R. Nikolas Macioci

For James Borders, a poet beyond compare and
a lifelong friend who always makes me laugh.

Acknowledgments

Grateful acknowledgment is made to the following publications in which some of these poems first appeared:

"Hospital Solace on a May Afternoon, 2024" *The Raven's Perch*

"The Apprentice's Self-Portrait" *The Raven's Perch*

"Standing in the Piazza San March" *The Raven's Perch*

"Stunned by a Spring Confession" *The Raven's Perch*

"The White, Wicker Rocking Chair" *The Raven's Perch*

Contents

PART ONE

Childhood is the kingdom where nobody dies.
-Edna St. Vincent Millay

There is a loneliness that only childhood knows.
-Unknown

HOW WILL I KNOW IF I'M AN ANGEL?

My Italian aunt, Mary Simmons pinned
a Catholic medal to my diaper
when I was born which Mom quickly
unpinned and threw away. Henceforth,
Catholic relatives lost the battle
to convert me. Dad didn't attend church,
and Father Joseph reprimanded him
whenever they passed each other
on Reeb Avenue where Saint Ladislas
Church stood like a beacon to Catholicism.
Mom, on the other hand, a Protestant,
claimed to be Lutheran and also never
attended church. Without a staunch
religious upbringing, my parents allowed
me to roam from one neighborhood
church to another.

On a particular Sunday, my nine-year-old
hand pulled open the door on Saint Ladislas's
rituals and I took communion. The wafer
on my tongue reminded me of the fish food
I fed my pet guppies.

A different Sunday found me singing hymns
in the Church of Christ on Innis Avenue.
Baptists scared me with their belief
in baptism by full body immersion.

By the time I reached twelve years old,
I had visited most of the churches
in the South End and concluded that
because all of them professed the truth,
not one of them was right. I was disillusioned
by confusion stemming from each religion
claiming to have discovered the truth.
How could there be so many different truths?
Each claimed more than the rest to be privy
to the words of God and Jesus. Declaring
superiority seemed like a game played
among different denominations, and
because I've never liked games, I stopped
attending all churches, decided by the time
I was fifteen that I was my own church.

Then there is the stone angel at the beginning
of the movie *Summer and Smoke*.
Her folded hands reach toward heaven
while fountain water pours down her torso.
It is as if she is importuning fate
for the ultimate answer just as I did
when I was young enough to think there was one.

THE BOY WHO STRAYED AMONG ADULTS

On this Saturday night, Mom, Dad, and friends
met at our house to play Texas Hold 'em.
I knew the name of the game from hearing
them repeat it so much. They loved cards.
The poker game lasted until midnight
then went into overtime because players
made clear they were having a good time.
All of them hunched over the kitchen table,
faces serious as death as they studied cards.

Occasional laughter and bursts of talk
awoke me. I slouched into the bathroom,
dampened a washcloth, wiped sleep
from my eyes and drooped into the kitchen.
They didn't seem surprised to see
a six year old standing in their midst
at that hour. I dropped into a rocking chair
across from their game, concentrated on
my next move, perplexed by not knowing
what little boys do when they awaken
after midnight. It was obvious
neither parent was going to put arms
around me and sway gently until I slept again.
My parents never expressed affection.
Eventually, I sagged into the living room,
flopped onto the couch, and drowsed
into a dream about being held
in very soft wings of an attentive,
caring bird that rescued me from
the inescapable detachment of adults.

FOILED AT THE TICKET BOOTH

The night I boarded a bus by myself
for the first time since I'd turned twelve,
rain sloshed around its mammoth tires
as if they were soaked in perpetual baptism.
Mom had just filed for divorce and celebrated
at a neighborhood bar. I had a dollar
in my pocket, an overwhelming desire
to see *The Greatest Show on Earth*,
at the Ohio Theater downtown, and freedom
to sneak away undetected. A risk, I knew,
but I tingled with anticipation to see that movie.
What if Mom came home before I returned?
I pushed that fear deeper into my mind,
fascinated with familiar streets zooming by
the bus window. On my own in this adventure,
I bloated with bravery.

As the bus approached downtown, shop lights,
streetlights, headlights stirred excitement
in my stomach. Rain decreased to drizzle
when I stepped from the bus at High Street and Town.
I hurried the half block to the theater.
Marquee lights shown like an illuminated welcome.
I stopped in front of the theater's facade,
eyes devouring the film's still shots
I wished I could take home and add to
my collection of newspaper clippings
advertising an array of movies.

I reached into my pocket for the dollar,
stepped to the ticket window, feeling guilty
as a robber. It was not a life-threatening moment,
but my heart thumped with an unexplainable fear
of being by myself downtown.
The middle-aged woman behind the glass
looked askance at me, wiry brown hair frizzed up
like antenna to detect boys who had left home
without permission, a watchdog woman.
I laid my dollar down. She asked my age.
I told her, and she snorted that I couldn't come in
unless accompanied by an adult. I shrank away,
reboarded the bus, enthusiasm dissolved
to disappointment, defeat smearing by the window
in soft focus.

SUNDAY BRUISES

I regarded Sunday as a paranoid plane trip,
slouched, a reluctant passenger strapped
into my seat watching the clock from hour
to hour. Eventually, I pulled the rip cord
on a psychological parachute that billowed,
puffed out, filled full of oppressing sky,
drifted me down to evening, and settled me
in a nest of paracords like a broken marionette.

As a kid, Sunday doldrums occurred
because it felt as if everyone, except my parents,
had stepped off the earth at the same time,
leaving me as if I were picnicking alone
in the backyard. Only gasoline stations
and movie theaters opened to the public.
Everything else closed tight as a lid
on a Mason jar.

Every Sunday, parents and I slumped
over a checkered tablecloth, eating
what seemed like the same mashed potatoes,
gravy, and pork roast every week. Although,
filled with food, I starved for company.
Neighborhood friends frittered away
most of the day in church or around similar tables,
obligated to spend time with family.

My house became hollow with silence
except for the upright, Philco radio
in front of which I sat cross-legged through *Superman*,
The Shadow, *House of Mystery*,
and various other favorites.
The radio functioned as my savior
in a personal church broadcast through airwaves,
a church in which imagination supplanted
the fixed questions and answers
of a God-fearing catechism.

PROOF OF LOVE

A wooden, Indian head plaque hangs
on the wall beside my single bed on
Barthman Avenue. Many nights, I focus
on it as I fall asleep, thinking how giving
the plaque is Mom's oblique way of
showing me love. She pushes away
from affection, has never hugged me
since I was a baby. If I put my arms
around her, she disengages as if from
a misplaced joke. Often, at night, when
I stare at the plaque, I think of death,
worry about the day I will lose my parents.
It's scary for an eight-year-old to have
these thoughts. I wonder if all eight-year-olds
worry about this kind of loss or if it's just
because my childhood has been disrupted
by abuse? My dad is a weekend drunk,
threatens Mom and me with knives and guns.

My parents own a confectionery.
Both of them work harder than Sisyphus
with the rock, but, as I've said, both of them
have failures, too. I've never thought
of running away, but Mom and I frequently hide
in her sister's house to escape Dad's mistreatment.
When I grow up and move into my own house,
I want to take the plaque to remind me
of a childhood fear that seemed unresolvable.

Seventy-four years later, the plaque hangs
on the wall of my study in Groveport,
a reminder of a past that was as emotionally hilly
as a roller-coaster ride. I no longer worry
about my parents' death because they've both
relaxed into a grave. Loss and grief have come
and gone like bad weather does. I'm used to empty
spaces where friends and family used to be.
I live by myself as alone as a late-night street.

YOUNG SORROW

I didn't run my hand over the silk
in the coffin lid, but I was tempted as
I stood peering down at the over-restored
face of John Marsh. Too much rouge
on his cheeks made him look as if
he was blushing from a risqué joke
told at an inappropriate time. I stared
because I was nine years old and
didn't know what else to do when looking
at a dead body.

It was the first time I'd ever seen a corpse
in someone's living room. Mom told me
the custom prevailed to keep the deceased
at home for viewing. I knew John's
seventeen-year-old face would haunt me.
It didn't look real. It resembled a plastic
mask purchasable in a five and ten cents store.

John had been a daily customer
in Mom and Dad's confectionery
on Barthman Avenue. He hung out there
with other boys his age. Four days ago,
a drunk driver lost control, smashed
head-on into John's Acme motorcycle,
practically decapitating the boy.

A group of his buddies formed
a kind of circle of grief, heads bent
like flowers on broken stems, mostly
silent as if their tongues had been cut out.
I knew all of them from the confectionary.
They served as my surrogate brothers,
teasing me, making me feel a little bit older.

John's death smeared a black mark
on all our lives. We would miss him
roaring to a stop in front of my parents' store,
his wisecracks crackling with good humor.

I flopped onto a chair near the wall,
pictured tomorrow when a hole in the earth
would receive his remains like a hungry mouth
swallowing him in one dark gulp.

DUST

I undressed to play doctor, became a willing patient.
Johnny Horvath, whose parents immigrated from Hungary,
talked with a slight accent.

One July afternoon, he invited me to his house
next to mine on Hinman Avenue. We had often
played together, climbed over the fence
to each other's property. I was six years old,
and he was a couple of years older.

We had never played in his garage, but on this day,
he wanted to show me the attic. We climbed steps
to a loft area in which an abandoned mattress lay
like an erotic invitation. He said he would be the doctor,
and I would be the patient. It felt strangely unreal
to be naked somewhere other than in my house.

We lay on the mattress, and his mouth explored me,
paid particular attention to my arousal. The attic
smelled of hot sunlight sifting like dust through
cracks in ceiling boards. Unbearable heat held us
in a sweaty grip as if it were a fur-lined animal.

Over the years, I've often thought about this episode
and how it was my initiation into sex.
I don't remember enjoying what we did.
My stance was primarily curiosity and a willingness
to tolerate his intention. If I had liked him more,
had he not been a bully, the experience
would have registered more positively. As it was,
I came away from that day mostly detached and mellow,
emotions that still surface when I think of Johnny Horvath.

AIN'T NOTHIN' BUT A SNOW DAY

Under covers, I wiggle deeper into warmth,
left hand reaching out for the on-off radio button.
I catch the last words of the announcer's sentence ...
"no school," listen for him to repeat. He says it
again. "Columbus Public Schools will be closed today."
My senior year at Marion-Franklin High School
has been blessed with a snow day. I can luxuriate
in extra hours of sleep, then call my two cousins,
Butch and Jim, who live on two acres abutting
my parents' two acres off Moler Road.
Since birth, Butch, Jim, and I have behaved
as if we were brothers. Anytime we find
an opportunity to be together, we grab it.

It snowed all night, and our fields are feet deep.
I bundle up in a hooded coat, tug on rubber boots,
slip my hands into fur-lined gloves. Snow pulls
at my feet, but I trudge onward until
I spot my cousins snowballing each other.
I join the battle, take a hit upside my head.
We pool our thoughts, decide to build a snow fort.
It's 1956, a time before the proliferation of drugs
ruined adolescence. We still maintained
an innocence that allowed us to believe
building a snow fort qualified as a significant
accomplishment. The snow rolled easily,
and after two hours of laborious effort,
we snapped photos of our new abode.

Late in the day, toward twilight, it began
to snow again, small flakes that Mom always said
accumulate. Maybe we'd get another snow day,
another chance to bask in the quiet nowhere
and purity of pre-adulthood.

PART TWO

The saddest thing in life is that the best part of life is in the past.
   -Ernest Hemmingway

Growing up is losing some illusions, in order to acquire others.
   -Virgina Woolf

DAZZLED BY NEARBY STARS

My memory flutters back to Summer of 1958.
I had been selected to represent Marion
Franklin High School as an apprentice
in the theater program at The Ohio State University.
Because my stepdad worked at the campus
print shop, every morning, he would drop me off
at gate ten of the stadium where a temporary
arena stage had been rigged.

Each week, I worked with a different crew:
makeup, costumes, lighting, and props.
Intense interest in acting unfurled in me
since infancy. I loved movies, and
when I was a preteen, I trotted ten blocks
every Saturday to the Russell Theater on Parsons Avenue
to absorb breathtaking magic flashing
from a matinee screen.

Afterwards, at dark, I would run ten blocks home,
careful to avoid riff raff and hoodlums who hovered
along Barthman Avenue. It was an easy price to pay
for the privilege of escaping childhood abuse
from my biological dad and entering a pretend world
for a few hours.

Last night of my apprenticeship, I strayed
through an opening that led to the playing field,
sat down in a folding seat, stared upward.
Stars looked like chips of mirror. I was 17.

Throughout the summer, I had been approached
sexually and romantically by various cast members
who assaulted my naivete. Some were television
personalities doing summer stock. On the last night
of my apprenticeship, I sat rigid as farewell,
overcome by vastness of the arena, the endless dark
of night, my own meditative aloneness. Behind me,
I could hear the muffled sound of an actor singing

"I Talk to the Trees" from Paint Your Wagon. I knew
at that moment I'd shed adolescent innocence,
didn't understand what kind of boy I had become,
but did suspect summer had matured me beyond the kid
who each morning rode to the stadium
in his stepdad's 1950 Ford, full of expectations,
sometimes listening to The Four Lads croon
"Enchanted Island" from the tinny radio,
not expecting life-altering experiences
just around the corner.

THE APPRENTICE'S SUMMER STORY

When I was 17, I ambled through gate ten
of The Ohio State University's football stadium
many times because I had been selected
by my high school to attend the University's
summer stock apprentice program.

Gate ten had been rigged as an arena theater,
an elevated platform open to the audience
on all sides. Although my responsibility lay
in working each week with a different aspect
of theater: props, scenery, costumes, lighting,
when I discovered *Life with Father* was going
to be cast, I couldn't resist. I got the part,
dyed my hair red, and joined my fictitious brothers
in the Day family.

The show opened to a rave review
about my portrayal of Clarence Day, Jr.
Sometimes, when I wasn't on stage, I would gaze
down from catwalks at the Fresnel loveliness
of Make-Believe. During the day, I painted flats
for *The Music Man*, sorted foundation makeup,
held incidental conversations with amateur
and semi-professional actors whose importance
seemed far removed from my meager accomplishment.
Their names, except for one, escape me now,
but he, I heard several months after apprenticeship,
had committed suicide. I knew it had nothing
to do with me, yet I recall one night while I stood

on the catwalk between scenes, watching the show,
he found me among shadows, fluttered his hand
to my thigh. I delicately refused, said nothing,
and left him in the darkness of his desire.

Over the years, I've thought about that incident,
decided his death indicated a failure to accept
who he was and his defeat in connecting
with the right person. It was 1958, not easy
to be gay. Such exposure to adults cured me
of adolescence. I swung from the youthful
trapeze of adulation. People called me handsome.
It seemed I would fly forever across center stage
netless, with music below me, satisfied
never to come down to earth again.

THE PARADISE CURSE

As a freshman in college, classmates and I
took numerous tests to see if we had
totalitarian tendencies. In the 1960s,
suspicion arose that everyone was inclined
to become a communist. The witch hunts
had begun again. I felt as if I were being
tried for witchcraft in 1692 Salem.
I had never danced with the Devil, but
since I rebelled against everything at that age,
he would have been a welcome partner.
I was as far away from totalitarianism
as Columbus, Ohio is from the Arctic.
I would not become the twenty-first one
executed, nor would my name appear
on the list of Salem's pardons. Ironically,
the devil would save me. We would conspire
 against ultra conservatives and the Joseph
 McCarthys. Art, and all its attendant
forms, would win. I believed all of this,
and so, when the professor assigned B.F.
Skinner's Walden Two, I was ready
to dismantle it page by page. Out
of a class of four hundred, the professor
said I was the only student who saw
the fallacy in Skinner's Utopia.
I'd always felt that I was not fodder
for a behaviorally controlled world.
His response didn't surprise me, but
I was alarmed that three hundred and

ninety-nine students were susceptible
to the idea, in fact, embraced it, that
they would have a better life in
a scientifically controlled Utopia.

On the last day of class, I collected
my term paper, beamed at the A+
written at the top, but I drooped
into the hallway a little despondent
that so many were willing to trade
dignity, freedom, and the human spirit
for a world in which a person is given
everything he wants.

NOW THE LEAVES ARE SINGING

Nedra probably had a crush on me
I didn't acknowledge. The pull between us,
however, seemed magnetic. For a while,
during sophomore year at The Ohio State
University, we sustained a close friendship.
Something intangible such as cosmic
inevitability drew us to each other.

We met in an American literature class,
liked some of the same authors, worshiped
Sherwood Anderson's *Winesburg Ohio*, and
agreed on many pet peeves about the instructor.
We wanted to tell him to shut up because
we thought we knew more about literature
than he did.

The indelible moment occurred during
an afternoon in early May. We had left
English class and were ambling down
a sidewalk that crossed the oval at the center
of the campus. In synchronicity, we folded
to our knees beneath a giant Oregon white oak,
then stretched out on the grass, leaning
on our elbows. Nedra began to sing
"Summertime" from *Porgy and Bess*.
The quality of her voice amazed me.
It resonated rich and clear. Although
her singing wasn't loud, the soft, melodious
sound drew compliments from passersby.

The whole scene felt magical, a spontaneous
experience that lasted only a short time.

When the semester ended, I never saw
Nedra again. It was as if she had been
the result of smoke and mirrors and not
a real person I had sat next to in English class.

Many years later, whenever I hear that song,
I see us lying under the giant oak,
smell the aroma of magnolia blossoms
wafting across the campus from Mirror Lake.

LLOYD PARKS

Lloyd Parks carried his soul in a briefcase,
worn, ragged, brown as a November leaf.
He instructed the Poetry Writing course
I took in 1960. Each day, eight of us
select students bent over a table, waiting
for the critical ax to fall upon our current
masterpiece.

Dr. Parks made me feel as if my talent soared
with promise. One afternoon, my current
assignment in his hand, he read through the poem,
stopped, reread the last line, said, "Now
that's music." Such praise astounded me,
subdued the other students, made me a star
for a while.

It was Dr. Parks himself, though, who daily
riveted my attention. Even at nineteen years old,
I felt a little sad to think the world had not yet
recognized his work. This was before I turned
middle-aged with a fiery need for the same kind
of recognition, realized the world may never
acknowledge my work either.

Now, in old age, I have never heard about
Lloyd Parks again, assume he did not succeed
in becoming the poet he wanted to be.
Such a thought dejects me, and even as I grow
older, I keep seeing him lug his beat-up briefcase
into class as if his whole life were in it,
hammered by unfortunate fate.

UNFORTUNATE LURE

I only knew I was good looking
when people told me. Otherwise,
I felt inferior. Over the course of my life,
I consulted six different plastic surgeons.
Each refused to do any work, said
I didn't need anything done.
This story is brief and takes place
when I was a freshman at The Ohio
State University. It seemed I dwelled
in a pocket of time wherein for the last
month I had been approached by various
men on the street who wanted to solicit sex.
I resented them, confused already
by questions about my sexual identity.
I endured the approaches, but inferiority
surfaced. I assumed something was
very wrong with me.

Anyway, this day on campus, as I rushed
toward my freshman, English class
in Denny Hall, I was ambling past
Mershon Auditorium when a middle-aged man
heading in the opposite direction stopped me,
said, "You know you're good looking, don't you?
I'd pay for you." I shrank inside, feeling
as if I were bait on a hook dangled
in front of a predator. Though not out
of the way, I detoured across the street,
continued toward class.

It was not the first time I'd been on this same edge.
The previous week, on an escalator in Lazarus
department store, a man stepped beside me,
accused me of being a tease. I had done nothing
to elicit that accusation. I was simply minding
my own business while riding the escalator
to the first floor. These incidents perplexed me,
and I found myself becoming self-conscious
about being in public.

Such occurrences became prevalent until
I reached my 30s. I concluded that
these lecherous men wanted my youth,
wanted to bask in my presence and
sip young broth from my body.
I was not flattered. They bothered me
with their licentious desires.

I'm old now, and although those times did not
disfigure me, they left me marked for life
with the opinion that I had certainly done
something wrong.

INFRINGEMENT

I didn't want to wear a monkey suit,
but I wanted the fifty-cents-per-hour job
as an usher at the RKO Palace Theater
in downtown Columbus. The manager,
John Stevens, hired me, and in a short time,
I adjusted to wearing the maroon outfit.
It was 1957, a time when I could carry
a flashlight down a dark movie aisle,
aim it at a disruptive patron and tell him
to be quiet. I also used the light to assist
customers to vacant seats. More often
than not, I lingered in the doorway
leading down an aisle and watched the current
movie. It was an on-your-feet job, and I tired
from standing so long.

One afternoon, the manager sent me
to the catacombs, a tunnel-like passage
entered through a door in the men's restroom.
He asked me to deliver a layout for a poster
to the resident artist who dwelled down there.
I shivered inwardly at the environs, creepy
as an underground cemetery. I found the artist,
a wizened, old man bent over a drawing board.
I handed him the layout. He stared at me,
reached between my legs. I dashed away,
hurried back to the men's restroom toward the lobby.
I was sixteen and too embarrassed
to report the incident. Instead, to collect myself,

I climbed up into the loft where the theater stored
pre-popped popcorn.

An hour later, I collected my first paycheck,
ambled to Flags shoe store, and bought
a pair of desert boots which, for the moment,
were in style and fashionable. I wore those boots
to the next gathering of high school buddies
whom I learned later wanted to bash me
for my arrogance as I strutted among them.
Even then, I kept my secret,
a discouraging mark on my young mind
like a question that asked why
I had been so susceptible to such wrongdoing?

SNOW BONES

The snow rolled into a ball perfectly.
It became the base. My brother, Michael,
rolled two more, one for the midsection
and one for the head. He wasn't trying
to build a unique snowman. He wanted
a traditional one, the kind pictured in
children's books and on greeting cards,
one with sticks for arms, dark pebbles
for mouth and eyes, a carrot nose, top hat,
pipe, and a wool scarf around the neck.

After he finished, I drove past to see
his creation. People walking their dogs
stopped, gawked at Michael's masterful
accomplishment. Of course, sun had
the last say about the snowman's existence.

Three gloomy days later, it warmed a little,
and beams of brightness broke from the sky.
The snowman softened; its life began to thaw,
became a distorted representation of itself.
Because snowmen don't have bones,
there would be no skeletal remains.

My brother and I have opposite personalities.
He's a Republican. I'm a Democrat.
He's conservative. I'm liberal.
He adores statistics and numbers. I hate math.
Despite these differences, we have stayed

connected. On this winter day, I'm thinking
of our relationship as a kind of snowman,
fragile, balanced, maybe susceptible
to dissolution under strong light.
I'm always surprised that the bond between
us hasn't melted. I can only assume
that the material of our blood tie
is much, much stronger than snow.

MESSAGE TO MYSELF ON MCGREGOR BAY

Sun, silent as a bird in flight, floods the shoreline,
brightens wooden walkways, reveals worn, dock pilings.
An early morning motorboat releases a wake that settles
into tiny waves. Pine trees squeeze life from rock,
seem without soil to feed on sky blue as the planet Neptune.

I'm spending two October weeks on Aunt Clara's Island
in Canada. Aunt Ada, Aunt Liz, brother Michael, Mom,
and my stepdad have also been invited by Mom's oldest sister.
I can hear them all awakening in various rooms of this white,
two-story house built in the 1930s atop the Island's rocky pinnacle.
Uncle Forest purchased the island with the first big money he made
producing airplane parts in the basement of his apartment in Dayton.
Eventually, he built a factory. Business thrived but did not preclude
a fatal heart attack in his forties. I praise him and his money
for indirectly buying me solace and the satin light that embraces
the island this morning. He was a very self-contained, standoffish
man who shied away from most people. Aunt Clara once told me
I was her favorite nephew. I have often wondered if I could have
become his favorite had time allowed.

In a few days I will leave this place. Intuition tells me I will
never return. From my second-story bedroom window
I gaze at the bay's panorama, harbor a desire to remain
in this place indefinitely. I pull on Levi shorts and a blue T-shirt,
grab breakfast, climb rocks behind the house for a better view
of the bay. I perch on an outcropping, compare water's intense blue

to that of the Aegean Sea, my mind already attempting to form language for an ineffable loss.

PASSAGES

A palm-size moon the color of salt
brightened the mid-July night as I waited

to board the Avalon, a ship that would take me
from Brindisi to Athens. Travelers queued

along the wharf, drooped tired heads, stared
wide-eyed out of sleepless faces. Reduced

to wrinkled clothes, forced wakefulness,
and tiresome balancing from foot to foot,

never had people looked so fatigued.
The ship's clerk, rooted to a chair

within a cubbyhole, stamped my ticket.
Above him, a sign reminded me to ready

my passport. I'd come from Rome, a day's worth
of train wheels still grinding in my ears.

From the top deck I looked down at a steward
standing in a doorway, hand grasping his crotch,

a signal to elicit my interest. I turned away
from the proposition toward my cabin.

I knew I wasn't coming back to find him later
the way light returns each day to awaken details

of the earth. Night pulled the ship forward
on an invisible towline toward Greece,

leading it into water deeper than understanding,
depravity, or the distance inward of human need.

PART THREE

Adults are obsolete children.
                                        -Dr. Seuss

Try to keep your soul young and quivering right up to old age.
                                        -George Sand

VOLUPTUOUS LIES

Who is this woman who sacrificed so much of me
for her own cause? This is the woman who
attempted to capture me with a net of possession
she mistakenly called love.

It all began the first year I taught in a small town
twenty-six miles from Columbus, Ohio.
Her brother; Ellis, was a student in my seventh grade
English class. He was enamored of my teaching,
asked his parents if he could invite me home for dinner.
I went as reluctantly as a dog pulling against its leash
because I knew he had an older sister, Josie,
who might be looking for a mate.

The dinner afforded all of us time to exchange amenities
and many laughs. I liked them. I liked her even more,
as a friend. She and I became close.

At the end of the school year, I took a job
as a tech writer in Galion, Ohio, an hour and a half away
from Columbus. I moved into an apartment
in German Village that abutted the neighborhood
in which I grew up. She, too, rented an apartment,
in front of mine. Since I worked out of town and
didn't return until 7:00 at night, I asked her to pay
a few local bills.

Months passed, and she assumed more and more
responsibility for my accounts. She paid my bills,
showered me with gifts, sent my poems to publishers.

One evening, she surprised me with news
that several of my poems had been accepted
by a prominent magazine and that the publisher
had arranged for film rights about me and my writing.

Eventually, the director of the film wanted to meet
me in person, arranged to come to town. Josie
ordered a sport coat for me from Hills Clothing Store.

So much had happened so quickly, in a matter of months,
that my family and I begin to feel uncomfortable
and suspicious.

One afternoon, I was visiting my Aunt Betty
who happened to have a friend working at Hills Clothing Store.
My aunt left the room to make a call to verify
the order. When she returned, her face paled.
She announced there was no such order. We looked
at each other, and all the puzzle pieces fell into place.
It was more like the proverbial domino had fallen causing
each consecutive one to fall also. Everything had been a lie.
All my bills had been unpaid. Josie had pushed
my charge accounts to maximum limits. There was
no Hollywood connection, and no poems had been accepted.
I left Aunt Betty tabulating each lie, decided
to pick Josie up at work and drive her to her family.
I didn't know if she was mentally ill or had just gone
to the extreme for me out of an uncontrollable passion.

We drove in silence. I didn't reveal my discovery
until we entered her parents' house and sat down
with the family to talk. After I told my story,
her mother simply said, "She did it all for you."

The response stunned me, and I left.
I never saw Josie again. I drove home thinking
about how I had been impaled on Josie's jagged illusions,
how constantly she had manipulated a chokehold on truth.

SUICIDE LOUNGE

I used to lay them out in the back room,
a space adjoined to my classroom.
The students represented poor families
and wealthy ones. The proliferation
of drugs in the 1970s captured headlines.
I don't know where the money came from,
but many of my students afforded the cost
of a high, a fix that sent them into
my metaphorical arms for help.
I became the safety net beneath
their drug-addled, tightrope walk.

The room behind my classroom held a sofa
and one chair. On occasion, an overdosed
student stumbled into my room, and
I would assist him to the sofa where
he would lie until recovered. Many
of these kids said they wanted to die.
It became my mission to convince them
otherwise. More than once, I talked
students out of self-murder, pointed out
that they were judging a life that hadn't
yet been lived, tried to sell them on the idea
that the next day would be better.
I succeeded, and no one ever died.
The ensuing drama, however, made me
realize how bereft they were of necessary
parental attention.

I had first taught in an urban school where
students' physical needs surfaced daily:
food, clothing, shelter. Later, as I moved
into a suburban middle school, I noted that
student needs were more psychological
than physical.

One afternoon, I slouched at my desk weary
from a day's worth of dealing with disposed
young people, remembered that I had someone
in the back room. I shook Adam awake
who seemed more stable than when I had taken him
back there. He appeared dazed that it was time
to go home, rose, thanked me, reluctant to return
to quick money in the pocket and hour after hour
of emotional neglect.

A BOUQUET OF BALLOONS

Cousin Sheila sent me twelve birthday cards
when I turned fifty. Whatever she did,
she did in excess. Instead of one gift,
when she arrived at my house to celebrate,
she dragged behind her a garbage bag filled
with presents. Moreover, in her left hand
she clutched a magnet from which sprouted
eight strings attached to eight, multicolored,
helium-filled balloons.

I had received for Christmas an early model
of a video camera. Shaped like a torpedo,
it probably weighed as much as one, but
I shouldered the unwieldy device and slumped
to the front yard. Sheila followed
with the array of balloons. The beautiful
April day afforded sky blue as a butterfly's
wings. The balloons bounced in the breeze
as I videoed her hanging onto the strings.
It was a picturesque tableau that resembled
a Norman Rockwell painting.

A week later, an unfortunate misunderstanding
overshadowed our relationship and ultimately
ended it. She had asked me to attend the family
reunion with her, but these were days I felt reclusive,
told her I didn't want to go. During the same week,
next-door neighbors asked me to go boating.
I accepted their invitation. Sheila found out,

roared with anger, wrote a five-page letter
in which she denounced me and terminated our
friendship. I never saw her again.

Thirty years later, I received a Facebook message
from her asking if I was her cousin. She confided
that a stroke had affected half her brain, and
she couldn't remember who I was,
asked for me to identify myself.
I never responded. Years ago,
it had been a perilous connection
with frequent ups and downs. Her temper flared
over the slightest thing which made it difficult
to get along with her. I didn't want to reconnect
or help her pick up the pieces of her life.
For thirty years, I had been free of aggravation,
free from her effort to possess me.
I allowed selfishness to rule my decision
and ignored her Facebook plea. Yet,
memory serves up that one particular day
in April when early spring warmed our backs
and she held onto the balloons to keep them
from flying out of sight and into oblivion.

HEART ATTACK DREAM

I awaken, dreams contaminated by realism.
I shambled down well-known streets,
Barthman Avenue as familiar as my childhood.
Heart failure, a bomb in my chest, ticked
like a threat of annihilation. Never making
a wrong turn, I stopped by the old confectionery
my parents ran in the 1950s long enough
to be depressed by its dilapidation, its ruination.
Chunks of missing stucco revealed cement block.
Front entrance, blocked by a sheet of plywood,
no longer admitted customers waiting
in a hot summer line for a dip of ice cream.

I turned down 6th Street, my limited time
a red truck on a vascular highway. I knew
I was headed toward Hinman Avenue,
a place to round out my life, a favorite residence
from early years. This is where I would die
in my dream. I entered the two-story house
built in the 1940s, started to panic
that there had been so many changes.
I lingered in the living room,
where we used to put the Christmas tree
near the staircase, when the same red truck flew
off a curve in the road, sped toward the sky.
Astral debris, like stars, shattered the windshield,
and everlasting night flapped at me
like a ripped, airless tire.

WHAT I LEARNED FROM ANOTHER'S LEGACY

I lug a basket of clothes from the clothesline
to the back porch, pull open the kitchen door
a carpenter friend, Randall, hung before he died
of lung cancer at age 45. The door's ill fit
sometimes requires me to press a knee against
its unfinished oak while at the same time
pulling it forward to get a tight closure.
I consider it a small inconvenience, find it
difficult to accuse him of faulty work.
I wonder how often Randall installed imperfect
doors? During winter, I roll a rug, wedge it
into space at the bottom of the door to keep cold
air from entering. How long had he been ill
and how ill was he when he cut and shaped my door?
I don't like judging him, but it's annoying to live
with defective workmanship. I assume
he had every intention of leaving a better example
of his craft. I drop the clothes basket in the kitchen,
wash my hands, saunter to my desk where I spot
an unfinished poem. I force the last line, in a hurry,
choose wrong words. I slump into a chair, study
the end of the piece, think about the door
and my own shortcomings in composing.
When I look at the legal pad, I take an unsatisfied
glimpse of myself and the fact that, like the carpenter,
I may die and leave behind work that falls short of
flawless excellence.

OMISSION

Tombstones in Bainbridge Cemetery,
located atop a hill overlooking route 56
that leads into the town of Bainbridge,
boil beneath July's seething sun. 102°
temperature should have kept me home,
but I struggle up the hill to take a picture
of a particular monument to use on
the front of my forthcoming book. To
my disgust, I find the monolith toppled.
I can't determine if the stone was upset
by vandals or age. My hand fans over
indecipherable writing, limestone smoothed
by irrevocable time. It's as if I'm trying
to feel discrepancy between being alive
and being part of the mystic void where
no amount of sun can resurrect.

I stand very still, anticipate a breeze
of which there is none, but I can smell
a mouth-watering scent of watermelon from
a nearby farmers' market.

I relatch the gate of the fence surrounding
the cemetery, grateful for temporary exclusion
from the dead. Yes, relief shoots down my chest
fast as a pheasant escaping a hunter's shot.
I am alive to coax meaning from another day,
to breathe one more exquisite breath. Behind me,
crooked tombstones point skyward

like tarnished slivers of tongue, and
if they could talk, would ask for their share
of eternity.

IN CHARGE OF THE DEAD

Some folks take fastidious care of graves,
plant flowers, shrubs, water, cut grass
away from the tombstone. I don't take
care of my parents' graves or any
of my closest relatives. I depend
on the groundskeeper for minimal
maintenance. I don't know what kind of
job he does because I don't visit.

If someone had told me twenty years ago
that I would behave this way, I would
have gasped at their inaccuracy. My beliefs
have changed. I think nothing exists
within my parents' coffins but empty exteriors.
I've taken their spirits into myself, and
I pay homage to that. I think, as a Buddhist
does, that after death, there is nothing
but an empty shell. The Toraja
of Sulawesi, however, keep bodies
of the deceased in their homes for as long
as a few years, believing that the line
between life and death blurs.

Life is petals on a rose, and when
those petals fall to the ground, nothing is left
but a useless stem.

The last time I visited my parents' grave,
soon after they were buried, ants had built
hills next to the footstone. They also swarmed
the marble. I sprayed the area with insecticide
as if the dead could actually be pestered,
never went back to see the results, assumed
the ants returned, oblivious of what lay beneath
their colonies.

BURIALS

Over the course of many years,
I watched each family member
lowered into a grave.
Without the air of hope,
bellows of my emotions collapsed,
flattened against my skull.
A cold layer of disbelief
froze the brain's skin
as I slumped away from
finality of many cemeteries.

ELIMINATING THE MATERIAL WORLD

Today, I'm getting rid of things I own,
no misgivings about preparing for death.
I'm keeping memories of laughter
and dust on marble windowsills. Otherwise,
I'll empty everything down to the core
of the room, having already given most
of my furniture to neighbors. A month ago, I
decided to clear the house of my belongings
to save my brother from having to do it
after I'm gone.

I glance out the window at a snowy scene
called winter. I'm battling with time itself,
sweating to shift things I know, things
I've accumulated, out of here: clothes,
tape recordings, books. I'm erasing
my signature from the cave wall, leaving
nothing to be discovered by new residents.
What good is stuff piled in dim corners:
trinkets, gadgets, gifts to celebrate
forgotten holidays. Some morning I will lie
on my heart the wrong way, twist it
into a conclusive end that will remove me
forever away from fads, collections, hobbies,
and an unceasing search for peace, or
will cancer and stroke vie for supremacy?

As I work, I grow strong about the task
of clearing out once-sacred items.

I tried to imbue life in lifeless things,
but nothing and nobody lived in this place
but me. I work with shirt sleeves rolled up
to my elbows, shuffle everything out
of the room into the trash.

After I've run the last carton of debris
to road's edge, I re-enter the house,
hang my coat on a basement-way hook,
look around as if I'm seeing the room
for the first time. I flop into the one
remaining chair, a wingback near the fireplace,
fold my hands on my lap, search
for what is gone. In all directions,
new space overwhelms, corpses of fake
immortality assumed from the possession
of things piled at curbside. Succumbing
many years to department store displays
won't delay my demise; purchases will outlast me.
I hope my extreme behavior in getting ready
for final closure isn't a cosmic embarrassment
as my articles and artifacts become souvenirs
for someone else's steadfast existence

PACKING AWAY EVERY INCH OF THE WORLD

I rise from a tangle of bed sheets
for the last time in your home.
It is as final between us as a drawer
being closed. I pack, remember
your early kindness from whatever
went deep into our lives, became
smaller, then disappeared like
a morning haze. I wouldn't call it
love. Temporary compatibility
is more accurate. You yelled,
"Get out," and I am, identical anger
a cue for leaving.

I trudge through a million, yellow
leaves, inside my head howl
"To hell with autumn."

Plodding into the night under
a burn of stars, I find an inexpensive
apartment wherein wallpaper has been
damaged by too much time, humidity,
and neglect. It is restorable,
unlike our relationship. I have no furniture.
I sleep on the bare floor, intend to shop
at Goodwill tomorrow. I close my eyes,
think how someone else will learn the secrets
of your body, take in your habits,
become familiar with what he feels
enclosed in your deceptive arms.

HANDSOME

If you're good-looking enough,
you can take liberties
with the world

A MELLOW DANCE AT 3 a.m.

Sandy, my former student, now a best friend,
and I had traveled to Morgantown, West Virginia
to attend a ceremony at the high school.
Earlier in the year, we judged the school's student
poetry contest. We wanted to be there in person
when winners received their awards.
Bags unpacked on the 6th floor of Hotel Morgan,
we freshened up a bit, left for the event.

Subsequently, we ate at the Iron Horse Tavern
directly across the street from the hotel,
returned to our suite and settled in for the night.
All of that was simply a preamble to what followed.

First, we read our own poetry to each other,
all the while sipping wine that Sandy had packed
in her suitcase. I had only one glass, but
Sandy continued to drink until
Apothic Red started to go to her head.
She tuned in to the music channel on TV,
wanted to dance and repeatedly bounced an invitation
off walls as if the room were full of potential partners.
I was half asleep on the sofa, eyes focused on her
almost mystical spinning. It seemed another self
had left her body, one that swayed, wobbled, whirled,
and twirled. Whitney Houston began to sing
"Run to You." Sandy sang with her, and
I was mesmerized by other worldliness of the moment.
Despite inebriation, for a little while,

my friend appeared insubstantial as a cobweb,
 a gossamer phantom capering about the floor
without a partner, generating her own personal grace.

OUTLAWS

My principal always sends me the rough ones,
students who are trouble for other teachers.
Today, Jerry shuffles into my room.
His alert, blue eyes beneath shadows
from black lashes, smile at me.
He sags to a lunch table I keep in my room
for Writer's Seminar, flops onto a chair,
wears worn-Levi confidence, feet ankle-deep
in the current sneaker trend, laces arranged
to look casual and uncaring. He smells of urine.

Once a month, he hangs out in my room
the entire school day, won't attend other classes.
I'm glad he likes me because he is one
of the leaders of the North-Side Outlaws,
an aggressive, hostile gang that rules
this side of town. For two years,
I assume I've provided a secure environment,
one in which he can claim his version
of going to school.

An unexpected revealment occurred
the day the principal scheduled a meeting
with Jerry's mom because his other teachers
were having fits about his absences and
unruly behavior when he was in attendance.
I opened the door to the principal's office,
gasped in surprise to see Barb, a one-time
student from my seventh-grade class years ago,

slumped in a chair, looking defeated.
I couldn't help but gasp, "How did you end up
with Jerry?" She looked at me nonplussed,
didn't answer. I was the only one
in the conference who wasn't having problems
with Jerry. I felt conspicuous that
I had no complaints against him unlike those
teachers who had requested a conference.

Afterwards, I ambled back to my room,
found Jerry sitting in the dark, head down
on folded arms. I switched on the lights.
He, of course, knew about the conference
and that his mom had been my former student.
He didn't say anything, shuffled toward the door,
threw a "See ya" over his shoulder, disappeared.
I never saw him again. Soon after,
police incarcerated the Outlaws, and I heard
from off the street that Jerry went to jail, too,
where he probably looked for a safe table
on which to rest his head.

UBIQUITOUS PROPOSITION OF FATE

It is a joke of desire
to be skin-close to someone
in the call of duty
but separated
by rules of conduct.

SENSITIVE MADNESS

You arrived in Columbus for a weekend
visit with a couple we had in common.
I lounged in a chair in their house when
you strolled in, astounded me with your youth,
an Adonis with whom I became immediately
infatuated. I wondered, even then, if I would
eventually be gouged to death, like Adonis,
by the boar of my fondness for you. We
connected instantly, rushed toward recognition
that we had both recently read Erich Fromm's
The Art of Loving.

Our unspoken romance existed
on an intellectual plane. Throughout
the evening, I was aware that I wanted more
from you than the treasures of your mind.
I wanted to lie down with you
for an indefinite time, feel your arms enclose
my solitude. That was never to happen.
You hinted that your brother had had a similar
relationship that ended in disaster. Is that why,
you seemed worlds away from any physical contact?

The evening ended with us exchanging
addresses and a promise to correspond.
You were off to Arabia, part of your life
adventure. During the next year, we sent
a couple of letters. I kept mine in the Bible,
reread them frequently. Time obliterated

intention, and I never heard from you
again after that year. The couple we had
in common said you had disappeared
from their lives, too.

Your brief presence imprinted my life
with unforgettable meaning. We called you
Cal, short for Calvin which means "bald,"
like the blatant truth of our feelings
for each other never openly expressed
throughout that evening or otherwise.

THE INWARD HOWL OF ISOLATION ON A SATURDAY NIGHT

When lights come on across the churchyard field,
illumination from vapor lamps and Kroger's sign,
two acres of vacant land take on shadowy darkness
opposed to the sable-black of night. I watch this
transformation from a dining room window.
My half acre connects to church property
which gives the impression I have more land
then I actually own.

I stare out the window as if I expected someone
by and by to trudge over the open area
toward my house. He would be a dim figure,
a silhouette bent on bringing me company
on a lonely Saturday night. I have not turned
on a lamp yet. I like to feel day evolve
into late hours. The transition dissolves everything
in the kitchen where I sit. Table, refrigerator, sink,
and cabinets disappear, and the black into which
I can see no reference point wraps me in fragile grace,
becomes the dark, longed-for arms that hold me
against the onslaught of suffocating solitude.

AVAILABILITY OF ROMANCE IN A NEIGHBORHOOD THEATER

Lights dim. The screen brightens with a studio logo.
It's 1974, a time when smoking prevailed in restrooms.
I saunter to the toilet. In the foyer, men loiter
along walls, cigarettes dangling from mouths
or between fingers like an appropriate prop.
Silence wins out, but ubiquitous glances flick from face
to face, established well-known signals intact.
I lean against a wall, retrieve a pack of Marlboros,
extract one, light it with a $4 Bic lighter.
I don't smoke, but it is part of the uniform required
to pass for an interested person and not an intruder.
All of us are as cautious as if we were shuffling down
a dark movie aisle. Other movie theaters like this
one exist throughout the city, theaters that have reached
the bottom of glamor and relegated to adult fare.
I suppose we are all alike in that we are trying
to look alluring in a subdued, masculine way, our stances
stiff with reluctance, but open to the invitation of a hookup.
I want to find someone with a glance who won't be lying
about his age, someone who may be lost from love but
willing to step out of the throng and claim we are not
like the others.

After an hour of pretension, I tire, stub out my cigarette, and exit.
Actually, I'm relieved not to have encumbered my life
with another person's story, or the confusion we both would feel
about how we're spending our lives.

I push open doors to mid-afternoon sunlight, bright
as the reflection off aluminum foil. I amble to my car,
glad to have turned my back on potential disappointment
and the possible consequences of high risk.

DREAM AS FLIGHT

"Lift me," I call to gravity. My purpose
is to fly through what is left of the dream,

to rise hollow as air, a hint of stars on my back
where I need feathers to be. Don't let me awaken

before I can spread my arms and open my eyes
next to hawks. Thermals widen under me.

My shadow parallels the earth, flat
as a sheet of paper. I dive, height falls behind me.

I look down at the ocean, a blue field where a ship,
like a tractor, plows furrows that sparkle with sunlight.

Before the dream splinters into fragments of awakening,
I try to land. Peering below, I aim for a safe place

to touch down. I lean into what is left of distance,
order myself to glide into a meadow full of wildflowers.

Beside me, on the ground within reach of my hand,
lies a broken mockingbird, its wings open too late,

its eyes yellow as a sunflower. Such death awakens me,
my tongue dry as dust, the room stuffed with remembrance.

HESITATION

The majority think you're a bad boy,
and from rumors I've heard over the years,
they may be right.

I've been invited to a friend's house
for a 4th of July get-together. You show up
unexpectedly, and a pall of rejection descends
upon the party like a black cloth over a coffin.
You've the kind of looks that attract admirers:
slim body, square jaw, facial features like
a Hollywood star. You seat yourself in the one
empty chair at my table. I have mixed feelings
about you sitting so close to me.

I haven't seen you since I met you years ago
at this same friend's house, another 4th-of-July
party when my crush on you began. At that time,
you were heading to Las Vegas to train
for a boxing career. I listened to you talk
about your goals and fanatical interest in boxing.
You were young enough to still have dreams
and motivation to fulfill them. All the while
you shared, I held you in my eyes as if
my eyes were arms. I became one of the subjects
of an old Frank Sinatra song, "I Fall in Love
too Easily." We didn't start any kind of relationship,
and I went away foolishly heartbroken
for no particular reason, daunted by infatuation.

And now, here you are again, looking more mature,
focusing on me wholly because I've always given you
complete attention. This time, it's not boxing
you talk about. I assume you've left that behind
as if losing tin cans from the back of a just-married car.
You elaborate on the paint business you've started,
have traveled to many states to offer services.
You show me pictures of your work. I'm impressed
with fastidious results. Maybe something is finally
happening good for you.

All through our conversation, I sense
an electrical pull between us. Hints
of unspoken, sexual attraction are
the proverbial elephant in the room,
conspicuous underpinnings that surface
when we look at each other.

I leave first, know that nothing will come
from our flesh touching in this goodbye
handshake and the reluctant dismissal
of possibility.

HUNT FOR THE WILD PEOPLE

The Garage, reputed to be the number one
gay-clubbing spot in Columbus, Ohio
during the 70s, drew a significant quantity
of straight people, too. It provided
a pleasurable environment and an exciting
atmosphere. Patrons exchanged friendly
conversations and frequent pats on the butt.

My first night there, I parked my brown
Ford Capri beneath a magnolia tree
in the parking lot behind the warehouse-like
building. Fruity aroma of May blossoms
permeated the air as I sauntered to the entrance.
I showed my ID and joined the throng.

A crowd as dense as that on opening day
at the Ohio State Fair mingled, bounced
to The Village People's "Y.M.C.A."
as I wound my way near the dance floor.
I never did frequent bars of any kind,
but this exception occurred because
I'd heard so many good reports about the place.
Most wore T-shirts and jeans or shorts. Of course,
bizarre exhibitionists flaunted here and there:
shirtless men, Hip-Huggers showing bare bellies,
and the sporadic queen decked in a feathered
headdress. Stereotypes abounded, to be sure,
but, overall, the population appeared dressed
collegiate-like.

I was bumping hips to Donna Summer's
"Hot Stuff" when I spotted him on the other side
of the dance floor, a fellow teacher
with whom I worked. He sported a white golf shirt
and dark-blue jeans. Our eyes locked,
and I assumed he asked the same question
I found in my head: "Is he gay or not?"
Brad, introverted as Carlie Bickford in *Jane Eyre*,
epitomized the shy, solitary individual.
He worked his way around to me.
We exchanged versions of hello.
The night ended in early morning
with me waking up beside him.

ORANGES HIDING IN A FOREST

I used to subscribe to *The New Yorker*
and often wrote poems influenced by
the magazine's unique, strange, and offbeat
covers. One such cover depicted oranges
hiding among a stand of trees. I scribbled
my poem on the white envelope in which
the magazine had been mailed, dropped
the envelope into a deep desk drawer
atop a pile of other jottings. That occurred
in 1990, thirty-four years ago.

Yesterday, June 27, 2024, I lifted
the foot-thick stack of yellow, legal pages
from the drawer, thinking it time
to do something with rough drafts.
Flipping through, I stumbled
upon the white envelope on which pencil
marks had faded. I read the poem, stymied
by what to think. What I felt, however,
amounted to a cold lump of disappointment
in my chest.

How did they do it, write poems
that an editor at *The New Yorker* considered
worthy of publication? My less-than-amateurish
poem made me cringe. The magazine existed
on an unattainable pinnacle, a citadel
in which special people and their special work
stayed unreachable.

I looked again at my poem and the picture
that motivated me to write,
crumpled the envelope, pitched it
into the wastebasket, turned my back
on oranges that would stay hidden forever.

AND NO ONE ELSE

I needed to escape home for a while.
Doldrums had set in like a predictable
headache. Sometimes, shopping brought me out
of the slump, so I pulled into Dollar General's lot.
The clerk, a frizzy-haired, middle-aged woman
with fifty pounds to lose, flashed a welcome smile
at my familiar face. I wanted toothpaste and aspirin,
but mostly, I wanted to be around people.

At various times, all my family, including
Mom's six sisters and three brothers, had died.
It was as if they were leaves that had fallen away
so easily from an October tree. I had one brother
who visited me once a week while his wife
attended Bible-study class. In essence,
I existed alone in a house inherited from parents
and much too big for me.

The aisles at Dollar General were obstructed
by unopened boxes. I had to wedge around them
to grab what I had come to purchase.
The store needed more help. It was evident
clerks couldn't wait on customers and stock
shelves too. Though cluttered, I felt cozy
in this place, but, after an hour of browsing,
thought it time to leave.

In the car, I tuned the radio to a little music
and laughter, leaned back against the headrest,
thought, "What now? Home, I guess."

Entering the kitchen, I thought about duties
I had neglected so that I could write:
table surfaces needed the compromise
of a dust rag. Loose boards on the back porch
had begun to squirm away from nails.
Maybe if I undertook these jobs, I would
feel less abandoned, less fragile living alone.

I glanced at the clock. 5:00 had come
as slowly as a worn-out, swayback horse.
I grabbed a plate from the cupboard,
a Budweiser from the refrigerator,
placed them on the table atop a green placemat,
not quite, but almost forgetting
about fate's betrayal and the bleak,
irreversible absence of family.

HOSPITAL SOLACE ON A MAY AFTERNOON, 2024

A bouquet of wires splays from the pocket
of my hospital gown, wires that connect me
to a heart monitor. I sit rigid in a plastic facsimile
of an overstuffed chair. Sheen of sunlight floods
the room through a window that runs the length
of the wall. Muted, intermittent blips of a distant
monitor punctuate an otherwise silent room.

I try to evaluate my life, wonder if heart failure
is a slow slide to the end. I study the room,
am overwhelmed by details: a single bed
with a knot of blankets piled at the foot,
a bedside table with a box of Kleenex and
a urine bottle containing two hundred milliliters
of saffron urine, an uncomfortable, gray couch
stiff as a coffin. Blue rubber gloves, a stack of
white towels lay on the sink top, ready to be grabbed
by a hasty nurse. I stare at a Walnut closet door
with two silver handles, think about how
God's failures have affected me for eighty-three years:
childhood exploited by an alcoholic dad,
the grueling social stigma of belonging
to a minority, a heart weakened at birth by rheumatic fever.
For the moment, my room is unattended by other people.
White walls accentuated by intermittent blue panels
remind me of the limited space I have been forced to live in
for the last four days. I want to go home

more than I wanted change left from money
Mom gave me to buy groceries at Cordel's corner store
when I was eight. I want to go home
to dishes that need washed, a floor that needs scrubbed,
and a dining room window smudged with the same sun
that warmed tribulations of my youth.

GETTING TOUGH WITH THE SUNSET

I haven't been to Palm's Pond for two years.
The pond can be found half a mile from my house

in Groveport, Ohio. Grasses, reeds, rushes,
and cattails surround the oval of water.

A one-half to three-quarter acre gravel path circles
the pond. I go there when I need a pleasant,

peaceful experience, when my melancholy overflows
with a yearning for things past. I prefer to arrive

at twilight, slouch on the wooden bench, stare
at the ball of sun as it melts below the horizon

like a fiery disk of orange sugar. Then, half-light
prevails, a dimness through which I can

still remember seeing a father and son packing
up fishing tackle, the dad's arm around the son's

shoulder, a tableau of affection
I've only known from a distance.

EVERYTHING ABOUT A BRIEF INFATUATION

My windshield blurs with rain. I rush
to the entrance of Barnes & Noble, step inside,
glimpse the clerk sitting at the cashier's desk.
He is as striking as a young man in a toothpaste ad.
I saunter toward rows of books, but maintain
a view of him as I pretend to look for a title.

When a store consultant approaches, asks
if she can help, I stutter out a random title.
She returns to her desk, consults a directory
to see if the book exists. I follow, glance
at the young man whenever I can, chastise myself
for wanting instant romance with a stranger.
He has already become a poem in my head,
a psychological wound from wanting something
out of reach. Why am I always weakened
by another man's beauty? Why am I embarrassed
by my own fantasies?

The woman says the book is not available
in the store but can be ordered. I thank her,
say I'll think about it. I pick up a copy
of *Writer's Digest*, head to checkout. I wait
three customers from him, think about
the frozen human within me, frightened
of the moment we will come face to face.
He sports a Joe Burrow NFL jersey, short,
brown hair glazed with product.

"Did you find everything you're looking for?"
he asks. Irony of his question stuns me.
I squeak out yes. Do the thousands of lonely,
Friday nights flood like ghost hymns from my voice?
Surrendering to the death of imagination,
the same death we hear about every Sunday
in church, I focus on the transaction.
He thanks me for my purchase, and I turn
to leave, wonder if he has graded me
as my seventh-grade teacher did when I trembled
at the chalkboard, feverish and wanting
to spell "desert" correctly and not "dessert."

NOTICE OF THE FINALE

I perch on a chair in the waiting room,
prim as if waiting in the foyer
of a funeral home, mind still stunned
by the news that my friend, Anna,
is dying of lung cancer. Her doctor
said there is nothing more he can do.
Hospice interceded yesterday.

Two women, both with carefully
arranged hair in bun fashion, idle
at desks behind glass shields, their jobs
supplanted by a kiosk. This lobby-like
space, quiet as a library, forces me
to confront remembered fragments
of time recently spent with Anna.

A couple of months ago, we traveled
from Columbus to Yellow Springs,
Ohio for a day-long getaway.
I snapped several pictures of her
sitting on a bench outside a gift shop.
Her rust-colored, pageboy haircut
gleamed in early May sunshine.
I posted that picture on the side
of my refrigerator, a reminder of
an almost perfect day.

News of her failing health has
hollowed me out as if a giant spoon
of fate scooped my insides to oblivion.
Empty seems to be the operative word
at this moment. I'm empty. The waiting
room is empty. My reservoir of hope
is empty. Into that emptiness, a nurse
calls my name, and I forget Anna
long enough to attend to my appointment
with a pulmonary doctor. It's not until
I leave the office that thoughts of her
come back to haunt, drift down over
my brain like a sticky web which
I am caught in until her journey
reaches an end.

THE WHITE, WICKER ROCKING CHAIR

Night's stars break through holes in the sky,
6000 thumb-size moons I gaze at fixedly
as if to escape smallness of myself
lounging in a white, wicker chair on the front porch.
I've never studied astronomy, know nothing
about mathematics of the subject.
I'm not a science-minded person.
I'm an aesthete longing to find beauty,
and the sky canopies my fulfillment.
Friends ask why I don't invite someone
to sit with me, share the sky. If I did,
I would feel I had betrayed a lover, literally.
I connect romantically with the sky.
I'm attracted to its androgynous embrace,
its steadfast and permanent availability.
I don't worry about it straying away from me
or becoming tired of my mediocrity.
I'm not jealous of its other doxies because
when I look upward, my interrelationship
feels singular.

I break away for a moment, sway back and forth
in the rocker, watch night become a deeper black,
wrap itself around my summer shoulders like a gift
from the Grim Reaper. There will be no more sky
after I'm gone. Heaven are these moments on the porch,
the indefinable vastness I am allowed to look at
as if fate had given me a sneak peek at eternity.

LIKING A DREAM TOO MUCH

An unexpected dream troubles me awake.
In it, I ambled onto the grounds of Clifton Mill
at Yellow Springs, Ohio, watched the over-shot
wheel convert natural water power into energy.
Fascinated and focused on the process,
I didn't sense the man in khaki shorts and green
golf shirt sidle up beside me. He stood so close
his sleeve brushed against my arm. We didn't speak
to each other. Physical proximity became our language,
an agreement to be together. I felt satisfied
for the first time in my life that I was making
a romantic connection, that someone had captured
my loneliness in a cage of soft acceptance. Immediately,
a woman pushing a stroller with an infant in it materialized
from nowhere, told the green-shirted man it was time to leave.

I awoke troubled that a moment of fulfillment
had been snatched away from me. The rest of the day,
the dream's aura hovered in my conscious mind.
I wanted to sleep again and dream a different ending
in which I felt it okay to encounter incidental attachment,
a dream in which seconds of tenderness might become
permanent intimacy.

SUMMER TRUTH

Bent at the elbow, my left arm rests
on the edge of the open car window.
Thermometer registers 96° Fahrenheit.
July is a drowsy dog on a steaming sidewalk,
reducing everyone to slow motion.
Sun seems as red as the stoplight I wait at
on my way to the grocery store.
The air conditioner quit working, so
I'm reduced to the whip of boiling air
around my neck. What scares me is
a summons in my blood to abandon this chore,
cruise the city, press down on another
person's passion until I feel
an alcoholic dizziness,
but I don't succumb.

I park in Kroger's lot, lock the car,
head to a cooler place. Afterwards, I turn
into my driveway, tug my sweat-soaked self
out of the car, unload groceries, haul them
into the kitchen. Later, ignoring danger
of exposing myself to savage heat,
I grab garden shears from the garage, snip grass
from flower beds, risk climbing a ladder
to strip off worn shingles from the roof.
I've never been so hot, but I continue
to go from task to task to displace growing desire
for the company of another person, the fulfillment

of eroticism that would take me to the streets,
expose me to numerous risks.

Returning the ladder to the garage, I thank myself
for staying home, squelching the inclination
for sexual fulfillment, think that many times
there is nothing better than the commonplace.

STUNNED BY A SPRING CONFESSION

Elbows pushed into your sides, you steady
the phone camera, step closer to where I sit
on a wooden bench in Schiller Park.
Your finger pushes the button to catch
only a suggestion of intimacy. You hand
my phone back to me, plop onto the bench.
I tell you I'm tired of taking pictures because
they leave out raw, negative emotion
flooding our relationship at this moment.
The camera does not see a confession
of your heroin addiction that you just unloaded
on me like a mountain of disparagement.
We sag silent on the bench, both of us clad
in Levi's worn thin as the leftover scrap
of commitment I feel after you admit
your drug dependency. The pond in front of us
glitters as if chips of gypsum have been sprinkled
over it. A child squats on the grassy bank,
pushes his sailboat forward with a long stick.
If he isn't careful, he will push the boat too far
away from shore to guide it, will have to run around
the periphery until it becomes close enough
for him to control again. The child affords
a common focus for us and my awkward effort
to communicate beyond shock. Afternoon,
May sky burns the eyes with startling blue
the color of a poison dart frog, it's color a warning
to predators that it is poisonous. You trudge
to the refreshments stand, carry back two Cokes.

Your beautiful hand slides down sweat
on the plastic cup. Droplets glitter like transparent,
minute flowers. I aim my mind's camera at you,
click a deep shutter, record the indecipherable image
of your secret and the death of us.

SEIZING REALITY

Tomorrow, I leave for a week's vacation
in Vancouver. I won't take my once beloved
camera because I'm past the point of taking
pictures of people and scenery, of capturing
a single second that no more records a whole
experience than one word represents a lifetime
of conversation. In place of my camera,
I pack a pen and legal pad. Photographs turn
the bigness of life into a lie, crucify it, nail it
to specificity, freeze a time, place, person
into a fictitious permanence devoid of emotion
and feelings known so well in the original
moment. On my trip, when I want to preserve
something of significance, I will flip open
my legal pad and write, capturing the nuance
of existence, a beautiful butterfly, in a net
of specificity and accurate language.

STANDING IN THE PIAZZA SAN MARCO

I close the guidebook, tuck it under an arm,
face St Mark's Basilica, believing our ancestors
generated faith through Art. Everywhere I look,

details of the facade glint sunlight off layers
of white marble. I stare at the domes made
of wood covered with lead. Five hundred

capitals and columns reach for the truth
of Heaven. The guidebook says this golden
cathedral houses the body of Saint Mark

the apostle brought from Alexandria and
after whom the city is named. It's here
that the world stays old. It wouldn't surprise

me, in this sacred atmosphere, to see angels
glide overhead through the drowsy afternoon.
The chandelier of sun dangles from sky's ceiling.

I wipe sweat from July heat off the back of my neck.
Yesterday, I toured the inside of the Basilica.
Today, I simply want to gawk at the brocade

of masonry, facets of imagination and engineering
that exude holiness. Several tour buses interrupt
my meditation, and I watch sightseers, backpackers

deboard in search of beauty. They, too, gape
at the glorious structure, the obsession of so many
workman's hands. They've come like paupers

expecting to be enriched by standing in proximity
to something majestic, something as
celestial as a city of saints.

GOD'S STARING AT ME

Most of the evening, I have pranced
from room to room, nervous as when a cop
drives behind me. Earlier in the day,
I had an impetuous urge to reread the story
of Adam and Eve, so from a drawer
in an antique washstand I retrieved
a worn book of Bible stories given to me
by Aunt Liz when I was a little boy.
Moreover, I reached for the King James
Bible and perused Genesis. Again,
the narrative fascinated me. I pictured
the serpent, coiled patience, waiting
for the infamous hand to reach out
for the extraordinary apple, red as blood.
One bite threw the world into chaos.

I shuffle into my bedroom.
Beneath a marble sill, a distressed, oak
cedar chest serves as a window seat.
I plop down, look out the window.
Fireflies punctuate August darkness,
yellow periods at the ends of night's sentences.

I didn't stop at Genesis but read further
in the Bible, found a tangle of do's and don'ts,
falderal of conflicting paths to salvation
and redemption. I concluded that
modern times necessitate not turning away
from the Bible but an overhaul, a rendition

that retains the Word but palliates outdated
beliefs and mores with common sense.
The Bible fails to recognize unavoidable
changes of an evolving world.

On the subject of sins, I have found my sins
to be as delicious as a hot fudge sundae,
as tempting as the need for a drink of water.
I never tried to resist opportunities to connect
with desires of the flesh. My greatest sin,
however, has been listening to self-righteous
people condemn me for being myself.
With an accumulation of wrongs and a plethora
of sins, I'm certain I've thrown myself out
of heaven's possibility.

PARAMETERS

You stand at the kitchen sink slathering
a piece of white bread with peanut butter.
I mosey up behind you, whisper in your ear,
"Did you wash your hands, make them clean
as blood?" This admonition, left over
from when my mom was alive and aimed
at me every time I entered the kitchen,
stays steadfast in my repertoire of habits.
You smile, answer yes.

We have retained a weekend relationship
without misery and serious sadness
for almost five years. Initially, I warned you
that most days I simply dress my nakedness
in language. I thought you may not understand,
but you have been supportive, appreciative
of my need to write poetry. Disappearing
to my desk has not distanced you from caring.

You plop into a seat at the kitchen table,
munch your peanut-butter bread. I fold
into a chair across from you, stare
at your beautiful face that doesn't realize
its own attractiveness. I never have to beg
or cry out for help because you have
always been ready to hear my poems and
to help me with clerical tasks.

Weekly, we follow the usual schedule
of two days together, Saturday and Sunday.
Come Monday, you shoulder an overnight bag,
and I began to feel bereft, your departure
a facsimile of loss pressed with a hot iron
into the successful fabric of our friendship.

THE UNLEASHED HURT

The principal has asked me to counsel
a student for whom the threat of suicide
is no longer a game. Silas outperforms
most of the students in his 9th grade,
advanced classes. He hides behind
sarcastic criticism and quippy jokes.
He's overweight, and his shoulders slump.

I wait outside the door of an office
I have appropriated for this meeting.
He shambles down the hall toward me,
and I wave him through the doorway
with a blur of my hand. Slumping
into a chair, he blurts a sardonic greeting:
"I see you're still working." I shoot back
with, " Now that I've seen you, I've resigned."
Despite the mordant exchange, We care
for one another, share mutual knowledge
and understanding that we both
had abusive childhoods. For some time,
I've been aware that he has wandered off
in pursuit of ruin.

His beautiful hands rest on his knees,
his spirit trapped by the past. I accept
the challenge, pull a chair a little closer to him.
His face seems drawn, lacking sleep.
I lead the conversation, lightweight at first,
long pauses, awkward silences. He knows

that I know his mind well enough to ascertain
his intention. The subject of self-destruction
lies between us like a deep ravine, not easy
for either of us to look into, both of us hesitant
to speak of it.

Finally, I tell him that self-inflicted death defies
logic, judges a life that has not yet been lived.
He listens, knows I make sense.

After an hour, we're past the hard part, and
I'm through trying to convince him to be in love
with life. He says, "Can I tell you something?"

I nod yes. Our eyes lock. His head tips to one side,
and I wonder if I've made a fool of myself trying
to be the best friend he has. He smiles through
his words, "I make fabulous spaghetti.
I'd like you to try it sometime."

THE HIDDEN MEANING OF GIVEAWAY

Hundreds of books surround four walls
of a basement room. Claustrophobia
does not attack me. Instead, it is as if
titles are eyes waiting to see which
of them I will choose. Mr. Feen has
invited me to view his library and
to select as many books as I want
to take home. It might be that he senses
the end, wants to clear shelves before
his demise. In any case, he bubbles
with enthusiasm since I show palpable
interest in his multitude of books.
History and biography dominate
shelves, fiction receives less attention.
He glows with delight when I choose
a chronicle of Ohio's development.
It could be raining as hard as a monsoon
outside or be as sunny as a beach-day
in Miami. Enclosed in the past
for these moments, we don't care
about anything beyond this room.
He shows me copies of "Letters
to the Editor" he wrote over the years
for *The Columbus Dispatch*. His
intelligence brims with stories, and
I listen with interest I once had as a kid
for programs broadcast from the upright
Philco radio. Although overwhelmed
with the number of choices I have,

I decide to take only one book because
I don't want to appear greedy or eager
to dismantle his life. Out of the corner
of my eye, just before I leave, I spot
a volume about the history of baseball.
Later, after I arrive home, I wish
I had taken that book for my brother
whose favorite sport is baseball.
Time spent with Mr. Feen in this
cloistered room is sacred. When I leave,
I feel as if I've spent a few hours in church
with a charismatic minister so much wiser than I.

PART FOUR

I am the family; face, flesh perishes, I live on.

-Thomas Hardy

*A family is a unit composed not only of children but
of men, women, an occasional animal, and the common cold.*

-Ogden Nash

BLISS

Family called it the little house
on Moler Road. Aunt Betty and Uncle
Clarence moved into it in the late 40s
from their home on Beech Street
in German Village. The little house
had one bath, a bedroom, a sizeable
living room, and a kitchen as narrow
as a diner in which if you bent over,
your butt touched the stove.

Out the back door, a half-acre of land,
also narrow, bloomed with a variety
of well-tended flowers, and a vegetable
garden that yielded enough produce
to supply Aunt Betty's sisters
with tomatoes throughout the summer.

At every opportunity, nephews, nieces
gravitated to Aunt Betty and Uncle Clarence
because this attractive couple exuded
youthful exuberance and a zest for adventure.
They played volleyball, badminton,
and croquet in the backyard, took time
to listen to the pangs of growing up
so prevalent in the younger set, and they sang.
Each month, they purchased a publication
that included song lyrics for all the current hits.
Often, they would break into song in the middle
of the living room or on a car ride. This is why

the young wanted to travel to events
with Aunt Betty and Uncle Clarence.
They attracted kids the way lantern light draws
June bugs. It was simply fun to be with them.

Uncle Clarence worked at the Columbus Plastics
Company on Mound Street. He started as
a stock-boy, eventually worked up
to vice president. It was during his climb
to success that he began to change.
He started to focus on accumulating money,
earned enough to move away from
the little place and contract the building
of a ranch-style dwelling farther down
Moler Road. Not only did he leave
the old house behind, but he relinquished
an irretrievable innocence. Aunt Betty
followed suit. They still attracted the young,
basked in the shadows of former selves.
It just wasn't the same.

More and more, Uncle Clarence became bitter,
seemed to resent the world. Aunt Betty
moved away from simple pleasures,
joined Clintonville Women's Club, started
to hang with people who aspired to become
members of the country club. Aunt Betty
and Uncle Clarence scarified purity
of their early lives for affluence.
They became a couple about whom
misgivings flared.

It has always been assumed that Uncle
Clarence felt chest pain during the night, struggled
from his bed, and plopped into his recliner
in the rec room. Aunt Betty found him
in the morning, head bent like a broken doll,
dead as his irrevocable past, a bloated, balding,
businessman.

Years later, on her deathbed, Aunt Betty,
referring to her wealth, questioned aloud,
"What was it all for?"

THE PRESENCE OF NEARLY FORGOTTEN REMNANTS

My brother built a pseudo table
under which Mom cowered during thunderstorms
and tornado warnings. Grandma Mohr
used to hide Mom in the closet during bad weather.
It was a hand-me-down fear that Mom attempted
to pass on to me, but I loved the drama of thunder,
lightning, and whirling winds. I could have been
a storm chaser. Zeus and I were conceivable friends.
I envied his thunderbolt. The makeshift table stood
in the west corner of the basement, served its purpose
well for years. Mom died in 2014, took fears of
an inclement climate with her.

The shelter comes to mind because I was
in the basement last week cleaning, looked over
in the corner, saw that table, now inaccessible
because of hospital equipment stored in front of it:
walker, wheelchair, cane, Mom's helpmates
as she became old and infirm. I stared at the items,
trying to figure out what to think. Remembering
wasn't a rifle shot to the brain, but an overwhelming
sadness oozed into my mind like a medicine
I didn't want to take. As I stood there,
the present felt bleak with loss. It was a mistake
to linger, so I strangled the urge to stare,
shuffled upstairs away from the broken self
seeing those items had caused.

WAY-OUT RELATIVES

I remember she had five new kittens.
They looked as if they were cookie-cutter cats,
all the same gray color. Violet, Mom's niece
and Violet's husband, Dwight, had decided to go
rural, bought a farm on the outskirts of Dayton.
Mom, Aunt Ada, Aunt Liz, my stepdad, and I
wanted to investigate this curious investment,
so one July morning, we headed to Bear Creek.

Violet, Dwight and the rest of the family
from that area we called the Dayton Crowd.
Impetuosity ruled this eccentric couple
who were known to pursue bizarre enterprises.
Last year, they became health enthusiasts,
visited us in Columbus with rags wrapped
around their foreheads. Dwight's dad practiced
medicine, and Dwight, an effeminate man
with bad breath, coasted along on a sizable
inheritance. Violet, wiry as a rabid monkey,
mouth puckered as if she'd just swallowed
sour news, qualified as a hypochondriac.

They weren't hospitable, exhibited a frigid
welcome as we parked on the gravel driveway.
Before I looked at them, my eyes went straight
to the cats. This couple couldn't be totally inhumane.
The extent of their farming amounted to owning
these cats because I didn't see any crops or
other animals. I gave this farming thing two years

at the most. Inside the brick abode, I didn't even spot
a Burpees seed catalog. Some farmers!
Violet gradually served lunchmeat sandwiches
and iced tea. My family's tongues hung out for a beer.

Mid-afternoon, having seen the so-called farm,
we gathered for goodbyes and left. On the way home,
observations and criticisms flew around inside the car
non-stop. We sighed with relief to have done our duty
by visiting, and we were contented to be away
from people whose eccentric behavior served
a sparse lunch and whose cold personalities were
more aloof than the stoics of ancient Rome.

PATIO

Uncle Heinie laid pavers end-to-end
until he had completed a square
large enough to serve as a patio
in the half-acre, side-yard of his and
Aunt Ada's house on Moler Road.
Upon the quasi patio, he placed a white,
wrought iron table with open filigree
and four matching chairs. A hole
in the center of the table accommodated
a metal pole at the top of which was
a metal umbrella. This was in the 50s
when their property still remained
uncontaminated by a deteriorating
neighborhood. Their estate was a showplace.

Each Friday, Mom, Aunt Liz, and Aunt Ada
carpooled to the grocery store. Afterwards,
they would lounge under the umbrella, sip
Budweiser. Why one particular Friday lingered
in my twelve-year-old mind, I can't explain, but it did.
The ladies wore dresses because it was not yet
the decade when screen-print blouses and stretch pants
without pockets replaced traditional garments.
I don't remember what two of them wore that Friday,
but Aunt Liz sported a white dress with black polka dots.
A white, pearl necklace encircled her throat.
It was the quintessential moment in her middle-age
of self-containment and self-satisfaction,
a time of trouble-free health before Alzheimer's
slipped into her mind like a treacherous jewel thief.

I snapped a picture of them that day lazing
under the umbrella. Aunt Liz stands out in her lively
dress and white pearls, oh those white pearls
that have become a symbol of a better time.

In 2024, the property and house have deteriorated
into a fenced-in ruin, the epitome of neglect, but
I have the white pearls, keep them in a bureau drawer.
They remind me of what was good
and what is past. In my hand, they rub
against each other, make a clicking sound
much like a defeated beetle falling to its back
on empty pavement.

GET 'UM DRUNK AND LET 'UM DANCE

The New Orleans Restoration Band tours
Ohio festivals during summer and fall.
Mom, Aunt Liz, Aunt Ada, and my stepdad,
follow this ragtime group of five musicians
from fete to fete. The Bratwurst Festival
in Bucyrus, the Popcorn Festival in Marion,
the festival at Saint Vincent's Church
off I-71 North, the Bainbridge Festival
of Leaves, and the VFW in Marysville
are places where the band plays each year,
places to where my family travels to hear
authentic Dixieland music.

At her home, when "Macho Man" blasts
from the radio, Aunt Ada springs
to her eighty-seven-year-old feet, dances
around the living room by herself.
At these festivals, when the band plays
"Darktown Strutters' Ball" or "Boogie
Woogie Bugle Boy," Aunt Liz and
Aunt Ada take the floor and jitterbug together.
The crowd eggs them on, applauding
the aunts' compatibility, skilled dancing,
and great show of enthusiasm. All through
these occasions, Bud Light flows and tipsy
dancers sway more and more.

During a 95° afternoon in August,
at the VFW in Marysville, misfortune
became Aunt Ada's final partner.
She was rollicking on the dance floor with
Aunt Liz to the "Clarinet Polka"
when pain flared in Aunt Ada's chest.
Musicians stopped playing and laid her
on the floor until the ambulance arrived.
Medics rushed her to Memorial Hospital
where several hours later her overworked
heart stopped beating forever.
She loved to dance, and she died doing one
of the things she liked and enjoyed the most.
Aunt Liz wept to have lost her sister and
lifelong friend, knew that at the next festival,
she would sit out the dance and step aside
for those fortunate enough to still have a partner.

A HAND-ME-DOWN GHOST STORY

I stare at a photo of the creepy house
on Graham Road where Mom lived
when she was a child. I found the picture
when I was looking through Mom's
old photo album. The snapshot had faded
almost beyond recognition. I restored it
in Photoshop, enlarged it, hung it
above the desk in the kitchen.

In the shot, the house looks as if
it is two houses, both sections connected
by a walkway. It's a winter scene, and
on either side of the house bare, tree limbs
reach skyward like skeletal arms.
I'm reminded of Heathcliff's abode
in *Wuthering Heights*. Grandma Mohr
insisted the house was cursed, claimed
she heard chains rattling in the wall.

The night the plaster ceiling fell
in the walkway, reminiscent of James
Thurber's tale "The Night the Bed Fell,"
everyone in the house came running
to investigate the commotion. Certainly
it was a supernatural sign that the house
really was doomed.

In the print, the mansion-like residence
does, indeed, look foreboding, not a place
in which I would want to live or even
spend the night.

I grew up hearing many times about
the house on Graham Road. As a little boy,
I felt spooked by Grandma's and Mom's
conviction that spectral spirits roamed therein
and that, consequently and without doubt,
the house was downright haunted.

STORY OF THE CLOUDS

Mom said when she was a kid, she used to lie
in the backyard on her back and watch clouds
change shapes. She saw sleeping dogs morph
into dragons, bouquets of white fluff become
one-of-a-kind creatures. Once, Abraham Lincoln's
face formed from a mass of cumulus
just before sunset.

As she grew a little older, she gave up
cloud watching and began charting her changing
looks in the bedroom mirror. Her strict dad
did not allow her to date, but occasionally,
she would sneak out the window, for a liaison
with the paperboy. Her dad prohibited makeup.

In preparation for one of her rare escapes,
she took a red leaf off an artificial plant, wetted it,
colored her sixteen-year-old lips in lieu of lipstick.

One night in July, heat as insufferable as a fire-walking
ritual in the Kalahari desert of Africa, her parents,
six sisters, and three brothers sprawled to sleep
on the floor near casements through which minimal breeze
entered. Past bedtime, Mom hoisted herself up
over the ledge of a living room window, dropped
legs down the other side and stepped upon her dad's head.
Commotion woke everyone who waited to see
the consequences. Her dad retrieved his belt,
waggled it at her without striking while

he locked her in her room. He seemed too stunned
by her boldness to punish a flagrant act of disobedience.
Penalizing would come tomorrow.

Mom later confided that she'd never seen a cloud
shaped like fear she felt at that moment,
a cloud as dark as the night she almost succeeded
in her risky caper.

PART FIVE

Everyone you meet is fighting a battle you know nothing about. Be kind. Always.

-Unknown

JOHN SLOAN SEARCHES ALONG ROUTE 317 FOR TEMPORARY INTIMACY

He ignores the dangers of hitchhiking,
parks his 1967 Camaro at a rest stop,
trudges five hundred feet to the highway,
lifts his thumb toward stars and
the possibility of connecting with a stranger.
Minutes after he feels gravel of the berm
roll beneath worn sneakers, a Chevy pickup
truck stops in front of him. He trots to the truck,
leans forearms on the window ledge.
The driver, a man perhaps in his early 30s,
asks "Where you headin'?" John answers,
"Anywhere you're headin'." The man smiles.
"Hop in." They ride in silence a few seconds
before the man comments that it's nice
weather for mid-October. Always a risk
to cruise, John thinks maybe he's safe this time.
"I own a farm just a few miles down the road.
You want to see it?" John says, "Sure."
Is this man an ax murderer disguised as a farmer?
John wonders.

They turn left off the highway onto a gravel lane
that leads toward a two-story, brick house typical
of farmhouses built in the late 1930s and 40s.
The side entrance leads into the kitchen, and
from there, they climb steps to the bedroom.
The chilly bedroom accommodates
an old-fashioned sleigh bed on top of which

a homemade quilt with hexagonal designs lays
like welcoming warmth. "I inherited this place
from my parents, and I live here alone.
No intention of marrying." They undress,
turn back the cover, slide into bed
from opposite sides. "Do you do this often,
pick up guys and bring them home?"
Wade wraps his arms around John. "You're
the first. Driving down the road, I couldn't stand
my solitude any longer. Saw you hitching,
took a chance that I could bring someone
decent home, have a little company for a change."
They forego sex, simply surrender to closeness,
hold each other in an embrace until morning
as if they have finally found a permanent
answer to loneliness.

JASPER WILKINSON

Jasper Wilkinson registered so high
on the attractiveness scale that it clouds
the issue to doubt whether or not
he should have been a model.
He was born beautiful, rode the school bus
with all the confidence I lacked.
I didn't look at his face much because
he always flopped onto a front seat,
being the second one on the bus, and I,
the first one on the bus, chose to perch
in the last seat and disappear
into inconspicuousness. Even
the back of his head drew my attention.
His crew cut added new meaning
to the word precise. Administration,
unaware of my crush, scheduled both of us
for the same 9th grade English class.

I rarely spoke to Jasper, feared approaching
someone so good looking. I had read once
that gorgeous people suffer from an unusual
kind of rejection because others are afraid
to go near them, so the comely suffer
a degree of social isolation. All through
high school, I kept a peripheral eye on Jasper.

Twenty-five years passed before I saw him again.
I had run to Bellman's, the corner grocery store,
to grab a few items, and he was clerking.
So much for the illustrious modeling career.
His bald head shined under fluorescent lighting.
I asked him how long he'd been working there?
He answered, "A week." He hadn't attended college,
quit the few factory jobs that hadn't satisfied him.
I couldn't help but notice his face had slackened
away from the pretty boy I remembered.
He said he'd read in the paper about my success
as a writer. I wished him well and left, musing
about his deterioration and unsuccess. I thought
about the many bus trips throughout the high school
years, convinced if I had to do it again, I'd slide
onto a seat in the front beside him, become friends
with his stunning looks before fate sabotaged
striking features with the beginning of hollow eyes
and jowls that hung nearly below the jawline.

FINALITY OF FLAMES

Johann Strauss II is dead.
His brothers, Eduard and Josef, have made

a pact that whichever one is left alive
will destroy the Strauss orchestral archives.

They fear that a competitor, Carl Michael Ziehrer,
will claim the Strauss family's works.

In April, 1870, Josef travels to Warsaw
for a series of concerts, collapses

on the conductor's podium, strikes his head,
and never regains consciousness.

His body is returned to his home in Vienna
where he dies five days later. According

to the agreement, the task of destroying
the family's works falls upon Eduard.

In 1907, he steps from his Ford Model R
Runabout in the Mariahilf district,

enters the furnace factory, carrying a valise
full of compositions. He opens the iron

furnace door, feeds each page to a blazing fire,
watches a lifetime of work incinerate to oblivion.

WALTZ IN DOUBLE TIME

Johann Strauss the first calls his son to him.
The son, Johann Strauss II, hides his violin
in the closet, slumps to his father.
The son has been sneaking lessons with
the first violinist of his father's orchestra.
Franz Amon teaches the seven-year-old
early in the morning before the Strauss
family awakens.

The son enters his father's study, shoulders
sagging with suspicion that he's been caught.
"I know what you're doing," snaps the father.
The boy hides his hands behind his back,
twists them into each other as if to squeeze
away stress. "I'm sorry, father. I'm sorry I
disobeyed." Johann the first replaces his pipe
in the pipe rack, clears his throat. "Come here,
boy, and bring me that switch from the closet."
The boy sniffles. " I'm really sorry, but
I want to play the violin. I'm sorry."
Reluctantly, the boy carries the switch to his father.
"Bend over, and quit sniveling." The two-minute
whipping is wasp stings on the boy's behind.
He sobs, "I'm sorry. I'm sorry." The father shouts
throughout the flogging, "I will beat the music
out of you, and you will become a banker. Now
go to your room and recover yourself, then
bring me the violin."

The boy sags to his room, takes the violin from hiding,
sinks onto the bed. He cradles the instrument
in his lap, runs a hand over its smooth surface,
hugs it to his chest against a shattered heart.

THE TIGER'S PAW

Adult sex shops have become our churches
Jordan thinks as he slinks into The Tiger's Paw
on the corner of Castaway Street and Elgart,
hoping no one familiar sees him. Musty
odor permeates the place as if it needs windows
opened to let in fresh air, but the only window
is the front one where a young man in his twenties
with a face full of piercings and tattoos perches
on a high stool like a beacon of security watching
for theft and cash customers. Three walls
of pornographic magazines and DVDs advertise
every imaginable lewd act to lure prurient consumers.

Jordan browses the magazines, looks over DVDs,
pretending interest, looking for a potential hookup
from the corner of his eye. A few other men scan
shelves, then disappear down basement steps
to peep- show booths that offer privacy and
a place for sexual activity. Jordan's testosterone
barometer has reached the bursting point.
He is hornier than the honeymoon fly,
the most sexually aroused of God's creatures.

Men continue to stream toward the basement.
Jordan gives up his pretense of shopping,
descends stairs. Hands on his glow-in-the-dark
watch point past 1:00 a.m., and the shop stays
open all night.

What he finds in the basement makes him gasp.
Instead of activity in booths, the basement area
itself accommodates one big orgy. At the center
of it, a naked woman allows herself to be fondled.
The men primarily cruise each other, but she is
the centerpiece for distraction until males find
affiliation with each other. Jordan unzips
his pants and instantly someone satisfies his need.

Afterwards, he ascends stairs, sweeps through
the shop, and exits into October's chill, relieved
to have escaped apprehension by an undercover
agent, the uncompromising noose of the law.

Back in his car, he promises himself never
to do this again, but as he drives away, knows he will.

REMARKABLE DEBRIS

He stepped out of the car, saw a bird bone
and a cigarette butt lying near the curb.
Had he discovered yin and yang in the gutter?
The Chinese would be offended by such
a thought, but he couldn't help note extremes
symbolized by the two items that lay at his feet.
What kind of bird belonged to the bone,
and who was the thoughtless person who flipped
the cigarette butt to the ground? These were
quintessential questions answerable only by
someone with creation in his fist.
He had found meaning in so little.

Moving on, he approached glass doors
leading to his cardiology appointment
on the second floor. Coincidentally, a nurse
wheeled a crippled lady toward the exit,
and he pressed the button to open the doors.
 "Your timing is perfect," the nurse said
to him through a smile. He felt heroic
as if he'd saved the day by opening
the doors for them.

When he reached the second floor,
the receptionist told him his appointment
had been canceled and rescheduled.
He was not angry. He was relieved
to be free of the obligation.

Back in the elevator, where three
sides were mirrors in which he must look
at himself unless he kept his head down,
he thought about bird bone and the cigarette butt.
They would still be beside his car, most likely
ignored by the multitude of people yet to park
in that space. Outside, the nurse and the
wheelchair patient lolled in the sun.
He didn't speak, strode straight to his car,
biggest questions of the universe unanswered,
nagging in the back of his head like the need
for a solution to the world's hardest math problem.

UNTENABLE ECSTASY

She was a rational woman by day,
but night darkened her motives, and
she became one of the highest priced
prostitutes in Columbus. Given her
level of income, she limited herself
to one client per evening. Josh,
her biracial son by a sailor who left
town on an aircraft carrier, wanted
his mom to stay home indefinitely.
She traveled elsewhere for most
of her appointments, but occasionally
brought a man home. When that happened,
Josh would clamp his bed pillow over
his head to dampen the sound of love-making
in the next room. He mostly raised himself,
roamed streets and alleys at all hours,
looking for treasure in trash barrels, hoping
to find a lucky charm that would change
his twelve-year-old life into that of a normal
child. He had known since he was six
what his mother did for a living, but
he ignored the truth, pretended she worked
as a supervisor in a warehouse not far
from where they lived in a middle-class apartment.

The day before his thirteenth birthday,
she brought a sailor home. Josh had never met
his father. The man paid particular attention
to the boy, asked about school, pastimes, and sports.

The man seemed genuine, and Josh appreciated
attention from an older male. The man and
his mom never went into the bedroom.
The three of them lounged in the living room
until a little after midnight. Left in the shadows,
Josh could hear their goodbyes in the foyer.
"I won't with the boy here," sailor whispered,
and then he left. Josh felt a warmth in his chest
as if he were sipping chamomile tea.
Maybe his lucky charm was working.

THE ONLY WORLD YOU'LL EVER KNOW

He promised to come back after he died,
and he did. Griffin and Floyd met
in elementary school, grew up together,
started a funeral home business conjointly.
They had always had a mutual fascination
with death, wanted to change human history
with an experiment. Whichever one
of them died first, he would attempt to
resuscitate, come back with a report
about what it was like to be dead.

One early May afternoon, Griffin's heart
stopped at the age of eighty-three. Lazarus
Syndrome, when the body imitates death,
excluded, Griffin's death stopped the heart,
bringing an irreversible end to his life.
Floyd forwent embalming, activated
an advanced defibrillator, a ventilator,
and other machines then covered Griffin's
body with a sheet and waited.

Floyd slumped by the autopsy table,
patient as if he were watching a garden grow.
When something stirred beneath the sheet,
Floyd whipped it back to reveal a groggy
Griffith who, with Floyd's help, struggled
to a sitting position. The question popped
from Floyd's mouth quick as a burst balloon.

"Well, what was it like?" Griffith blinked
to further awaken himself. "Nothing.
There is nothing afterwards. No heaven.
No hell. No pearly gates. Nothing.
Not even darkness." Floyd blurted out,
"This will change whole histories of religions
and their various catechisms. It may even
cause people to worship the moment.
Wobbly, but able to walk, Griffin slid
from the table, stood, and with a slight smirk
of satisfaction, said, "Let's go for a beer
and enjoy the world while we're alive."

JUVENILE TYRANNY

Buzz Atkins, tough enough to wear glass
in his back pocket, rips the scab from a bruise.
He doesn't believe in Band-Aids. His bullying
shadow hangs over most of the kids
in the neighborhood like a phantom menace.
Some, more than his age, have tried to subdue
his browbeating and fisticuffs, but he threatens
them by flattening bicycle tires and noses.
His bulk itself is an ultimatum: chest and biceps
overdeveloped from lifting weights. He pushes
from behind causing kids to skin knees.
Of course, his frontal attacks, equally harmful,
land victims on the sidewalk. Periodically,
he throws firecrackers at dogs, floats stray cats
in the bathtub until the last fatal moment.

Adults speculate whether or not he will outgrow
brutality. Parents are leery of allowing
their children to hang around Buzz, but
kids have strategies for finding their way
to each other.

Everything changed the day Martin Souder
moved into one side of a double on 6th Street.
Kids and adults soon learned that Martin,
though built like a miniature tank, bully material
to be sure, functioned as an eleven-year-old
peacemaker.

The showdown occurred one mid-August
afternoon in front of Martin's house.
A group had gathered around Buzz who was
cutting legs off a praying mantis with
cuticle scissors. Martin flew from his house
to investigate the commotion. "How would you
like your legs cut off," Martin spat at Buzz.
"Try it," Buzz challenged. Martin punctuated
the exchange with a punch to Buzz's stomach.
Buzz flattened against the pavement, scissors
flew into the street, and cheers from the crowd
went up like flags of surrender. Martin's
heroic move brought forth pats on the back.
Thus began a new adolescent government
in this formerly intimidating milieu.

NIGHT PARADE

Vacant-eyed men pose against the brick wall
of a homeowner's terrace on the corner
of Jefferson and North High Street.
They've come to hook up with drivers
who keep circling the block like desperate
merry-go-round horses. Some of these loiters
work as hustlers. Others want a quick sexual fix.
Anonymity prevails.

John Walters wears Levi's with a twelve-inch flare
at the bottom, a white T-shirt, and Donny Osmond's
1970s hair. A pack of Marlboros nests in his
rolled-up sleeve. He doesn't smoke, but
the cigarettes serve as a convincing prop.

It is nearly 1:00 a.m. when the phantom blue
Monte Carlo pulls to the curb and beckons him.
A bald, chubby man rolls down the window, asks,
"What you up to?" John answers, "Not much."
"Wanna go for a ride?" the driver questions.
John opens the door and slides onto the seat.
His twenty-five-year-old mind calculates the risk, but
the worm of sexual need has crawled into his gut.
The man steers toward Upper Arlington, parks
in a garage attached to an impressive,
expensive-looking home. He directs John
through the kitchen to the basement door,
descends steps to a bed that seems to wait

for carnal coupling. They strip, lie together
touching parallel flesh. It's clear that
the man wants to worship John because
his mouth consumes the young man. For two hours,
the corpulent gentleman cannibalizes John,
or so it seems.

It's nearly 5:00 a.m. when they return to the wall,
July night still dark enough to see stars blink.
John, now a safe distance from harm,
accelerates home.

BEACH VENDOR

He parks his food truck 100 yards from the Atlantic
among an array of bodies with oiled limbs.
It is as if he is in a garden of flesh that hungers for sun
from a savage sky. He opens a serving window,
hears gulls overhead, sees them dive toward a wave
the size of a redwood tree. A few preparatory moves
and he begins to welcome customers, feed the public,
host the hungry, the foolish, the arrogant, the humble.

Lines of bathers and beach bums aim spears of their
appetites at him, impale him on impatience.
Over and over, he scoops ice into cups, fills them
with Coke. As quick as the talk of a traveling salesman,
he readies hot dogs and hamburgers. Odor of cooked
onions wafts from the truck, mixes with ethereal breezes
from the sea. Occasionally, he tightens his apron,
a painter's smock, smeared with splotches of mustard
and ketchup. Youngsters splash from water, head in
his direction, their arms and legs a bit wobbly
from too much horseplay. Somewhere, from the crowd,
a radio blasts Taylor Swift's " Who's Afraid
of Little Old Me?" When there is a rare lull in business,
the vendor glimpses gulls that continue to fly and dive,
ravenous as peckish people who wait in line.
He turns around, reaches for the ice cream dipper,
isolation of his job continuing to give rise to loneliness,
solitude, sadness within the confines of this one-man truck.

TRUE PASSION IS ABOMINABLE

"Laugh" is a dangerous word
when you've decided to end existence,
when you've called on all the angels
to see if you've missed even the slightest
answers to life's inevitable questions.
You harbored impetuous dreams as a youth,
wanted to feel a second heartbeat, your own
and someone else's in the same body.
In adulthood, you dress well, but the human
connection you hunger for dwindled
to no more than the tailored suit that carries
the shape of your bones around from day to day.
As your teeth rot, you want early years again.
You want freedom from trivial matters
of your livelihood because business has become
an unceasing bore. Nothing seems to exist
but pointless routines from morning to sundown.
You dreamed about justice and every kind of peace
to no avail. Now, with briefcase under an arm
and arms close to your sides, you hurl yourself
down metaphorical stairs, relinquish your grip
on surrounding air, fly off the earth
with every kind of unfulfilled desire intact.

A BRIEF GLIMPSE INTO THE BARREN LIFE OF A PICKUP

In the restroom of the hotel, she stares
into the mirror, frustrated with her aging face,
reapplies flame-red lipstick, blots her mouth
with a tissue. Back at the bar, she slides
onto a stool, orders a Jack and Coke, thinks
if the Budweiser sign behind the bartender's
head were edible, she would love the taste
of neon. This frivolous thought supplants
a memory of the last man with which
she walked out of here. They had met twice
subsequently, and he had been late both times,
had sent roses later as an apology.
She never saw him again after that.

She sips her drink, wonders who will sit down
beside her to offer smooth, opening lines.
Eventually, a stranger does perch beside her.
She smiles at him. He buys her a drink.
They exchange introductions. He appears to be
years younger than she, sports a green, golf shirt
and medium-blue Levi's. Soon, his invitation
lifts her from her seat, his eyes seeming to separate
dense warmth of bar bodies, making a path
toward the door. He is a minor character
behind a cigarette glow, knows his part too well,
allows her to go first as if he were performing
a piece of stage business. They amble to his black
Accord, the spring evening a redemptive lyric
ripe with sexual anticipation and the fragrance
of nearby lilac bushes.

BLUFFS OF ITHACA

Odysseus scuds toward shore,
his skiff aimed at the island of Scheria.
Athena tows him from water
into a world rearranged
by his ten-year absence.
His hair, silvered by time, shines
like a helmet of light. His eyes,
blue as off-island depths,
stare for recognition,
search for Penelope, Telemachus,
the son he left behind
as if in abandonment.
So he can discover Penelope's suitors
and seek revenge, Athena's magic
disguises him as a beggar.
His raw and rueful presence resolves
changes that have occurred.
He competes in the trial of the bow, wins,
identity restored, resumes his rightful place
as king of Ithaca. Thereafter, he
and Penelope wade daily along the shore
of the Ionian Sea, gulls skimming the surface,
love without end permanent
as the indestructible sun.

DRESSED TO PROVOKE THE PURCHASE OF LOVE

Sharon dabs on light touches of blue
eyeshadow, applies black mascara to lashes.
In panties and bra, she pulls up a short skirt,
slips into high heels to make herself look taller.
It is time to pretend she is not in her own body.
It is time to pretend she is not repulsed by a client.
She will spread her legs and listen to husbands
yak about their pregnant wives or the fact
that they tolerate a relationship in which sex
is no longer available. Afterwards,
she will scrub herself clean and cuddle
her three-year-old son who will never know
what his mother does to bring in money.

Daily, she remembers the fatal phone call
during which she learned that her husband,
slouched in an office chair, viewing business
activities at Bushman's corporate office,
had died of a heart attack.

The night is as dark as her pimp, Rudy,
who wears a ring on each finger
of his right hand, quasi brass knuckles
to keep his wives in line. Sharon has never
experienced his violence because
she is as obedient as a well-trained child.
After her husband's death, she turned
to the streets because she didn't think

she could make more than a meager wage
doing anything else.

Rudy drops her at the door of her client,
a rich man in his sixties whose spouse is
spontaneously having an affair
with a former student. Joe, whose bald head
shines like a polished stone, invites her in,
and if eyes could salivate, his would be slobbering
at the sight of her. Joe is her only client
for this night, and he leaves $2,000
in an envelope placed on the coffee table.
She retrieves the money after an hour's work.
Rudy picks her up, takes his share of the earnings,
drops her off at her house.

The twenty-year-old babysitter is asleep
on the sofa. Sharon shuffles into her son's bedroom,
gazes at his slumbering form, holds him to her heart
in imaginary arms.

EXQUISITE

You gaze out from La Jolla Cove at the Pacific,
a blue garden in which mysteries of marine life grow.

A yellow swimsuit marks tan lines, and you imagine
a nude beach where you can even out the color of your body.

That, however, is of no immediate concern. You've come
to see dolphins. They do not disappoint. White-sided

and an occasional bottlenose loop from the water, point
heavenward for a second, their backs polished by sunlight.

They bring friendship as close to the shore as they dare.
You ache a little to touch one, but they dive deep,

too far from your hand. Satisfied with what you've seen,
you turn away, slog to a cabana, change into street clothes.

You will not come back again to see the dolphins. Tomorrow
morning, you will board a plane for Columbus, Ohio where

no smooth dolphins will rise over and over from the sea
as if in perpetual resurrections. Tomorrow, you will

resume mundane tasks, walk streets of the earth
to find something as ethereal as you did at La Jolla Cove.

BERLIN DAVIS'S GUIDE TO SELF ENCHANTMENT

He bends toward a block of light gray marble,
focuses exacting eyes, a patient hand drawing
layout lines with a pencil. He will sketch in
Oscar Wilde's line, "Where there is sorrow
there is holy ground." Later, he will etch in
the epigraph's permanent words, forgo
sandblasting, the modern approach that involves
using compressed air to shoot small particles
of sand through a hose to cut the stone, and
resort to a hammer and chisel, tools he learned
to utilize during his three-year apprenticeship
that started when he was seventeen. Now,
at twenty-seven and a master craftsman,
Berlin acknowledges his success results
from working in the shadow of Joe Gibbons,
a monumental engraver and owner
of Gibbins Tombstone Company where
Berlin has worked since his apprenticeship.
He has never felt morbid spending his days
around tombstones. They are the catalyst
for his creative output, objects of artistic
achievement. Not unlike a graphic artist
or a painter, his objective is to produce
something of beauty.

He focuses intensely on this project
to meet the month-long deadline.
Before he reaches an end, he will use
chisels, files, calipers, and mallets,
implements that help him bring his profound
vision from the stone. During many,
late hours, he will push and pull
tones and shades from the marble.
He will achieve an admirable outcome,
because he is an artist whose ultimate
goal is no less than a reach for perfection.

THE SERIAL-KILLER WALTZ

The Shaw family murdered their only son
with church dictates and the poison of
self-righteous superiority. It wasn't
a homicide with blood and clearly discernible
evidence. Insidious exclusion became
a prime weapon. Rodney was gay, and
they minimized his existence by failing
to invite him to family events. Little by little
he shrank into himself, became quiet, withdrawn,
and almost invisible.

The Shaw family attended church regularly,
had swallowed sermons wholesale like
a tempting meal. In their minds, they were
doing society a favor by eliminating their son
and anyone else like him who followed suit.
They didn't consider themselves assassins
but prided themselves on their ability
to rear a good, Christian boy who, in spite
of their admonitions, had gone wrong.

Rodney didn't actualize his sexual preferences,
but his parents worried that someday he would
embarrass them all by loving someone of whom
they did not approve. It was risky to keep him alive.
Had they been lucky, he would have committed
suicide, but he was stubborn enough to hang onto
life in a shadowy way. That meant the Shaws
had to devise a plan that eradicated him

as a family member. No rides in the family boat,
no invitations to family dinners, no holiday
celebrations or birthday parties became necessary
for permanent removal of this forty-six-year-old man.

In due course, one autumn afternoon, Rodney died
from complications related to diabetes, but
as yellow and red leaves flew past October windows,
truth is that he'd already been dead,
daunted by religious dictates and family alienation.

THIS IS NOT THE PLANET HE IMAGINED IT TO BE

Obb renamed himself Aphidids,
the name of a Medieval alchemist
Obb found when he browsed 14th century
Arab history along with other histories
in preparation to teleport from his planet,
Empathos, to the blue planet. Alphidius
seems a viable moniker; since Earthlings
would, having a penchant for nicknames,
probably call him Al. After studying
the entire planet, he chose Waynesville,
Ohio as his destination, population 5,858,
just enough to substantiate his inquiry
into why humans embrace destruction.

Only one hotel exists in Waynesville.
Al takes the sixth-floor suite. After donning
a white T-shirt and jeans, American's favorite
uniform, he strolls down Main Street.
What is a Dairy Queen? he wonders.
Opening the door, he enters away from July
heat. Cold confections seemed to be
the dessert du jour. His English, learned
from signals sent into space for a hundred years,
is perfect. He orders a cone of vanilla,
tastes its sugary sweetness, doesn't discern
any sign of negative behavior, so he ambles on
down Main Street. Maybe the Flower Boutique

will afford insight into why mortals behave
destructively.

Chris greets him. Her fifty-two-year-old fingers
twist wire around gladiolus stalks. Al looks
in shock at the cut stems. On Empathos,
they never cut flowers. There, fields overflow
with flowers, and none are ever cut.
He looks around the shop, appalled to see cut flowers
in freezers, vases, arrangements. "Why
do you cut them?" he asks. For a second,
Chris hesitates. "To make beautiful things,"
she answers. "But they're beautiful when
they're growing. When you cut them, they die."
She pushes the gladiolus stems into floral foam.
"Death represents change. Everything must
have an end for a beginning to exist."
Al thanks her, satisfied to have learned the answer.

LOGAN VANCE INVENTS SUNLIGHT

When he was six, he fell in love with the sun.
Light beams streaking through a dining room
window onto flowered carpet reminded him
of warm arms holding him safely away from
parents' quarrels.

At age twenty, he continued to need the uplift
of light to offset residual trauma
from his parents' divorce, so he rented a cabin
in a faraway place. Mount Thor, located
on Baffin Island, Canada, the world's most
vertical cliff with a 105-degree overhang,
afforded Logan sufficient privacy.

Many late nights, he forced himself to stay
awake until morning, focused fully
on his laborious task. Bent over
a solar simulator, a device that replicates
natural sunlight in a controlled laboratory
setting, he pushed its potential beyond limits,
augmented its power with his own ingenuity.
The ability of a solar simulator to approximate
natural sunlight is based on three criteria:
spectral match, spacial non-conformity,
and temporal instability. Logan aspired
to displace the criteria with a simpler and
more immediate solution. He wanted more
control than the simulator allowed.

After two years of concentrated effort,
he discovered a solution, a one- button variation
of the simulator that produced sunbeams exactly
like the ones that had rescued him from a dismal
childhood in the dining room years ago.
With the push of one orange button, yellowish
streams of light flooded the lab,
made welcoming patches of brightness on the floor.
He was safe again, would hereafter be embraced
by yet bigger arms, cosmic ones.

SIX-PACK SYMPHONY

Tog Britten chewed Husky smokeless tobacco,
tongue pushing a wad into his sixteen-year-old jaw.
He lived with parents and three older, bully brothers
in Little Oklahoma, a small, shabby community
with rundown houses off South High Street
in Columbus, Ohio. Tog's mesomorph body,
lean but muscular, threatened smaller boys,
and he liked it that way. He did not work.
His parents allowed him to freeload off them.
They did not restrict his wrongdoing
or offensive behavior. In essence,
he was rearing himself with the help of
street buddies.

He and his fourteen-year-old girlfriend, Louise,
had fooled around enough that she had
recently become pregnant. This scared Tog,
but it didn't nullify his self-centeredness.
He would find a solution, and
everything would be under his control again.

The answer came to him on a late October
evening at 9:30. He would rob Griff' Grocery,
grab enough money to afford Louise's abortion.
He borrowed a Glock 19: 9mm handgun from
a friend who owed Tog money for a bag of cocaine.
Griff stuttered, had an unsteady hand
because of shock to his nervous system

while serving in Afghanistan. At forty-five,
he hoped to retire by sixty.

The October night felt balmy to Tog,
but he needed a jacket's inside pocket for the gun.
Griff had seen Tog often enough to identify him
as a neighborhood brat, a troublemaker.
Tog stepped to the cash register, ordered
a six pack of Coors. Griff huffed, "You're not old
enough." Tog pulled the gun and answered
"Will this convince you?" Griff whipped a Beretta
from beneath the counter, aimed at Tog's heart,
service training intact. Tog collapsed to the floor,
a trickle of tobacco juice dribbled from his mouth
like brown water from a dirty river.

LOGAN BECOMES DANGEROUS

Sunday dinner at his parents' house consisted
of pot roast, creamed peas, mashed potatoes,
gravy, and salad. His mom, stepdad, and brother
slouched around the dining room table,
bent over their food as if lost in prayer.
Sparse conversation consisted mostly of
pass me this or pass me that. Tension had reached
a breaking point like a rubber band stretched too tight.
Logan's legs wiggled under the table,
a habit that kicked in when he became edgy
or excessively nervous.

For months, his parents had hinted about him
being gay, but a showdown conversation
or confrontation had not yet occurred. Instead,
his parents tormented him with suggestive
discourse. His mom had told him
it wasn't healthy for a boy to spend so much time
in the bathroom. One Saturday morning,
his stepdad had pulled off spark plug wires
so Logan couldn't drive his car anywhere
suspicious.

Dinner proceeded until his mom said,
"You're messing with your hair too much lately."
Without warning, a violent sweep of his arm
sailed his full plate of food against the wall.
Gravy dripped down flowered Waltex.
A glob of mashed potatoes dropped to the floor.

Logan immediately felt guilty and contrite,
regretted his fierce reaction, but it was too late.
He had made his unretractable statement,
pushed his chair away from the table,
and fled the house.

He drove south for an hour, trying to calm down.
Scenery rushed by, but he hardly saw it.
His mind, partially blurred, questioned why
his life had to be so hard.

Twenty-five miles from Columbus,
he pulled down the rural driveway
to his aunt's summer cabin. He didn't
have a key, so he curled up on the back seat
until he collected himself. It was 1966.
He was twenty-years old, still lived at home.
In a while, he would return and suffer
consequences. Nothing would be said,
and he would go on living with undivulged truth
and nothing brought to light but an overall
sadness that shrouded the house like a fragile web.

BIG, STRONG, AND WITHOUT SYMPATHY

Curtis, a Social Studies teacher,
controlled audio-visual equipment
housed in a small closet attached to the backroom
of the Linden McKinley High School library.
Teachers who wanted to use any equipment
were required to fill out a form in advance
of the period during which they wanted
a projector, recorder, microphones, etcetera.

Curtis would push his beer belly out,
bully any teacher who made a request.
Administration granted him several periods
during which to handle audio-visual responsibilities.
His gruff voice challenged anyone attempting
to hold a conversation with him. Unpleasant,
uncooperative, and intimidating exemplified
his best characteristics. He was a cigar-smoking
tyrant from Texas.

A pathway through the backroom of the library
led to the school's outer hallways.
Students often took the shortcut. Some lingered,
regarding the room as a place to hang out.
Curtis had the disgusting habit of touching students
inappropriately. Buttocks qualified as a favorite target.
He didn't discriminate between boys and girls, although
females appeared to be his prime prey. Many knew
about his perverse behavior, but no one ever reported him.

He simply existed as part of the school's goings-on,
a crusty, middle-age man who during his whole career
slipped through the cracks of reprobation.

THE OTHER SKY

Aerobatic maneuvers fill the sky
with jet planes that appear to have gone haywire.
Navy Blue Angels, Thunderbirds, F-16 Fighting
Falcons, Boeing F/A-18 Hornets flash overhead
scorched by sun, vroom through clouds
tearing them into white pieces of misty haze.

Brian Culbertson flies his Edge 540
at full throttle, pulls the plane into a 45 degree
up line, rolls it inverted. He lets go
of the elevator stick, sees if the plane can track
the line for a few hundred feet before leveling off.
It's a beautiful move, an action that elicits wows
from the air-show audience.

In particular, a twelve-year-old boy in the stands
gasps with appreciation and amazement.
Oliver's recently divorced mom collected enough
money to purchase tickets for this event.
She didn't want to disappoint her son who aspires
to become a pilot.

After the show, Oliver wedges through the crowd
toward the airfield gate, spots Brian, waves to him.
Brian crosses the air strip to autograph Oliver's program
asks, "Are you going to be an airman someday?"
Oliver answers, "Yes," his smile, half the width
of his face, a grin of gratitude for his adventurous hero.

That night, Oliver sleeps in the cockpit of possibility,
flying farther away than stars.

I'D RATHER BE FAMOUS THAN UNDERSTOOD

Based on an incident described in *The Secret Life of Salvador Dali* written by Salvador Dali

I linger at the top of steep, stone stairs
leading outside to the recreation area.
Students and supervisors at Maris
Brothers' School in Figueras
glance at me with suspicion. I've dawdled
too long not to raise a question about motive.
Stray students stream around me, quizzical
looks on their faces, probably wondering why
I haven't joined the others yet.
This plan came to me last night, and
I will follow through regardless of outcome.

I wait until the yard is full of people, and
after much hesitancy, I leap, land halfway down
the stairs, rebound like a basketball to the bottom,
bang myself up pretty bad. I have no doubt
by morning, I'll be bruised all over and hurt
as if I've fallen out of an airplane.

Everyone comes running. Boys, superiors gather
around me. Someone lays a wet handkerchief
on my forehead, I'm astounded by all the attention,
satisfied by the result of my ploy. Never
have I had so many eyes upon me.
It feels as if hundreds are looking.

My sixteen-year-old ego swells.
I've lived too solitary, been shy, reclusive.
I blush at even meager attention.
A different self crumpled at the bottom
of the stairs, a self exalted and triumphant.
I experience happiness unlike any
I've ever known, and tomorrow
I will jump again as if the whole world waits
to see me do it.

BROKEN SOUNDS OF A COLD WOMAN

She dwells in a house of maximum quiet,
does not turn on the TV or radio.
Only the furnace and refrigerator cycling
disturb the void. Agneta, a Scandinavian
name meaning pure and holy, reaches for
a paper plate on which she will serve herself
tuna noodle casserole. She favors iced tea
the year around. She did not celebrate
her 64th birthday last week, an age beyond
the range when most people marry.
Her parents disfavored marriage,
including their own, preached against it
vehemently. They had come to dislike
each other enough to part, but stayed
together to raise Agneta.

She lives a regimented life ordered
and organized as if it has been overseen
by an army's drill instructor. She won't
admit that she wants someone's love,
often laments the loss of the only man
she ever dated a year after high school.
He wanted intimacy. She frowned upon
the idea as if it were an unpleasant odor,
said she would only submit if married.
She told her only brother, Martin,
to bury her in a white dress as proof
of her virginity.

Agneta reads much, prefers mysteries,
hates romance novels. She unwelcomes
anyone at her door, carries on long conversations
with a telephone friend from high school.
That epitomizes the extent of her socializing.

She carries her plate of casserole to the dining room.
Lack of companions, she eats alone every night.
Finished, she throws away her paper plate, reads
for a couple hours, then goes to bed at exactly 10:00,
neither five minutes before nor five minutes after,
pulls the chain on the bedside lamp.
The room disappears into darkness much as she has
in the throes of self-annihilation.

THE RAIN DOESN'T STOP HERE ANYMORE

Luke notices winds have shifted. A monsoon
will follow. First raindrops spot his newly
washed Kia Optima parked outside his apartment
in Sukhumvit. A retired stockbroker at Merrill,
he moved to Bangkok at age fifty-four.
He likes the city for its restaurants and nightlife,
occasionally visits Nana Plaza, a naughty district
reputed to be the largest red-light complex
in the world. During his five years of residency,
he has never, however, dropped into the Q Bar
or the luxurious Bed Supperclub.

As a bachelor, he lives a solitary lifestyle
with the exception of the few friends he made
during his first year in Bangkok. He and Boon Mee
have dinner together at least once a week
at Akira Back which is where they first met.

Rain increases to a downpour. He's reminded of
The Rains of Ranchipur, a 1950s film in which
unrelenting rain caused much destruction.
Luke peers out a living room window, sees
through a curtain of water that the city has turned
gauzy, indistinct. Because of 95° July heat
and insufferable humidity, he has decided to stay
inside until evening.

He knows rain will continue until September.
The first year that he lived in Sukhumvit
he thought the constant rain would drive him
to an insane asylum. By the end of the monsoon,
he had learned to live with the constant deluge,
thought it somewhat comforting to be cocooned
by persistent, round-the-clock precipitation.
It was like being held in watery arms.
That thought makes him consider going
to Nana Plaza later despite weather. There,
he can assuage loneliness, pay for one of the girls
whose arms will assuredly not be made of rain.

THE APPRENTICE'S SELF-PORTRAIT

His mentor stands aside, stolid as ice,
patient, waiting for the next brush stroke.
The boy dabs detail, angles his head
to assess perspective. In his mind,
paint is luminous as words that would roll
from his tongue and sing in a voice
not yet a man's. The easel stands
at the side of the room near a window
where July sun is at its brightest.
The boy is unsure of his next move
because the mentor has taught him
empty spaces and silences count.
The mentor steps toward the painting,
shadows a touch on the boy's shoulder.
The boy turns a hesitant smile toward
the older man. The finished painting
is a near perfect representation
of the boy's seventeen-year-old face,
handsome as Antinous, and, like Hadrian,
the boy is the mentor's weakness.
They share an embrace of attitudes,
agree on the painting's success.
To celebrate the end of an apprenticeship,
the mentor brings out a bottle of Lambrusco.
Even though the boy has not reached drinking age,
the occasion warrants a social violation,
and so the wine is poured, wets each of their lips
like a surrogate kiss.

PART SIX

These fragments I have shored against my ruins.

-T. S. Eliot

EASY SPRING

The rock of winter rolls away,
and we come out resurrected,
count on daffodil and crocus
to appear. Being human
weighs on us with fastidious
promise, a necessary sensation
of being mortal. The urge
to live forever surfaces
as we study new sky,
blue as a morning glory.
We push aside difficult pain,
wend through fragile grasses,
bodies robed in golden sunlight.
Clouds, white as Arctic wolves,
hang low, shift shapes on a hook
of breeze. In back alleys of despair,
hard eyes of gamblers watch
their dice give up a few more
uncertainties while we, in the open,
bask within sureness
of the season's return.

LEAF SHOW

Sometimes a day is as perfect as cashmere
or a quiet morning. Such was the afternoon

my friend, Liz, and I traveled to Buckeye
Lake, Ohio for a getaway and to see October

foliage. I parked the Ford Capri off the road
in front of a farm located between the lake

and the canal that ran perpendicular.
The canal water reminded me of army camouflage,

greenish brown, impervious to sun's rays.
Mom's parents used to own a college

on this canal, and we visited once a week
for years. The golden day glowed like the tail

of a giant firefly. Flawless, Uranus-blue sky
emitted an occasional gull. We slid from the car,

ambled toward a giant oak. The tree was alive
with yellow brightness, each leaf a piece of sunlight.

We stood beneath its branches, saffron radiance
cloaking us as if we were wearing an autumn garment.

Arranging ourselves for a close-up, I snapped
several selfies. Satisfied with the results,

we settled back into the car. Even now,
ten years later, I still feel the burn of sun

that day, remember the trip home past trees
aflame with orange, yellow, red and a hint

of purple, a wildfire of color, believed
at the time there was no better place to be.

ABOUT CORN

My friend and I ate sweet corn for dinner,
lathered it with butter yellow as liquid sun,
seasoned it with snow grains of salt.
We consumed two ears each. As he collected
our plates of empty cobs, I asked him
if he'd ever thought about the person
who first pulled an ear of corn from a stalk
and roasted it. Who was that person?
On what day of the year did it happen?
What season was it? Was he alone in a field
of maize and suddenly got the idea to eat corn?
I had ignited my curiosity. My friend bent
over the sink, washing dishes when I Googled
about the entity known as a fruit, vegetable,
or grain. I found astounding facts: corn is
not natural. It is man-made. Nine thousand
years ago in the lowlands of west-central Mexico,
native people in the region bred the wild grass
teosinte to create the first edible corn.
Native Americans brought corn up the Mississippi
River. This information fascinated me, and
I continued to read about how important corn is
to our culture. It provides the primary energy
source for livestock, but to my surprise,
discovered other little-known ways in which
it is used. I called my friend away from the sink,
asked him to sit down and listen to some fascinating
information. He slid into a chair across from me
I began to recite: "You will be flabbergasted to learn

corn is used in toilet paper, drywall, toothpaste,
crayons, diapers, spark plugs, soap and hand
sanitizer, aspirin, rubber tires, and fireworks,
not to mention cereal, salad dressing, ice cream,
and candy." My friend seemed astounded, amazed
by these facts. "Have we been eating something
as valuable as gold?" He asked. "I think so,"
I answered, shook my head in disbelief, reiterated:
"Just think," I said, "it all started with a wild grass plant."

CORN SHOW

Henry A. Wallace, aged sixteen, ambles
up to the judge's table, asks if he may
speak to the judge in charge. "I am he,"
answers a man in a gray, three-piece suit,
sack coat, waistcoat, and trousers.
"What can I do for you?" Henry asks
how the judge will know if the Blue
Ribbon winner, if planted the following
Year, will produce a higher yield than
the ears that did not win a ribbon.
The judge shuffles his feet, stammers
an explanation with which Henry
does not agree.

Henry returns home, begins his first
experiment by planting seed from 25
award-winning ears and 25 ears that
were marked the poorest at the corn show.

In time, on a sunny October afternoon,
he collects data from the three-acre plot
located in his backyard. Results show
that the highest yielding corn did not
come from an award-winning ear but
came from an ear near the bottom
of the rankings. His experiment proved
there is no relationship between
the appearance of the ears and yield.

Years later, Franklin D. Roosevelt appoints
Henry vice president of the United States
and makes him secretary of agriculture.

Henry stands at a window in the White House,
remembers the moment he challenged
the corn show judge, thinks he hasn't done
too badly for an Iowa farm boy
with a pocket full of seeds and
a head full of determination.

WHEREABOUTS OF RED

A ruby-colored swatch of light washes the
sky at sundown, a crimson souvenir of a day

almost past. A heart, removed from my chest
during cardiac surgery, lies in a tray of blood.

Bringing the first plague against the Egyptians,
Moses raises his staff, turns the Nile River scarlet.

Plumage of the northern cardinal, symbol of energy,
passion, and courage, fluffs in a breeze. Soluble

pigments of strawberries ripen in mid-June.
Roses, tomatoes, the robin's breast suffuse summer.

Beneath a streetlamp, rouged cheeks of a prostitute
brighten. Flames radiate from a fireplace, luminosity

tinging walls. The innards of a watermelon spill out
with the cut of a knife. Leaving all traffic behind,

a fire engine streaks to its destination. Melting down
to a stubby wick, the red Christmas candle burns

to extinction. Loose maple leaves, autumn ornaments,
decorate the air. Crawling over ocean floors, lobsters

sometimes cannibalize smaller lobsters.
Red is the color of light with the longest wavelength

in the visible spectrum. Red is love, passion, and danger.
If eaten, the fly agaric fungus can kill. If eaten,

its red mushroom shape with white dots, causes
hallucinations, drug sensations that induce sleepiness,

dizziness, delirium, and the black promise of poetry.

9 789363 542907